WORKBOOK
with Digital Pack

1

CEFR
A2

TH!NK
SECOND EDITION

Herbert Puchta,
Jeff Stranks &
Peter Lewis-Jones
with Clare Kennedy

CAMBRIDGE
UNIVERSITY PRESS

ACKNOWLEDGEMENTS

Author

The authors and publishers acknowledge the following sources of copyright material and are grateful for the permissions granted. While every effort has been made, it has not always been possible to identify the sources of all the material used, or to trace all copyright holders. If any omissions are brought to our notice, we will be happy to include the appropriate acknowledgements on reprinting and in the next update to the digital edition, as applicable.

Key: W = Welcome, U = Unit.

Text

Joshua Silver for the text in Unit 7, Copyright © Joshua Silver. Reproduced with kind permission; Kenneth Shinozuka for the text in Unit 7, Copyright © Kenneth Shinozuka. Reproduced with kind permission.

Photographs

All the photographs are sourced from Getty Images.

W: Sonsedska/iStock/Getty Images Plus; NosUA/iStock/Getty Images Plus; UmbertoPantalone/iStock/Getty Images Plus; Tpopova/iStock/Getty Images Plus; VladislavStarozhilov/iStock/Getty Images Plus; satapatms/iStock/Getty Images Plus; Henvry/iStock/Getty Images Plus; Ittipol Nampochai/EyeEm; **U1:** SelectStock/Vetta; MarioGuti/E+; Raquel Lonas/Moment Open; Hill Street Studios/DigitalVision; miodrag ignjatovic/E+; William Thomas Cain/Stringer/ Getty Images News; **U2:** Floortje/iStock/Getty Images Plus; LeventKonuk/ iStock/Getty Images Plus; modustollens/iStock/Getty Images Plus; Gearstd/ iStock/Getty Images Plus; Rose_Carson/iStock/Getty Images Plus; Creative Crop/DigitalVision; sigridgombert/RooM; Ian Hooton/Science Photo Library/ Science Photo Library; Jose Luis Pelaez Inc/DigitalVision; Janifest/iStock/Getty Images Plus; Steven Morris Photography/Photolibrary/Getty Images Plus; Dorling Kindersley/Dorling Kindersley/Getty Images Plus; kertlis/E+; firina/iStock/Getty Images Plus; popovaphoto/iStock/Getty Images Plus; Coprid/iStock/Getty Images Plus; Florian Haas/EyeEm; Hero Images; zeljkosantrac/iStock/Getty Images Plus; Fuse/Corbis; Pornpawit Phosawang/EyeEm; skodonnell/iStock/Getty Images Plus; bns124/E+; Alberto Manuel Urosa Toledano/Moment; Nathan Blaney/ Photodisc; **U3:** Floortje/E+; Assja/iStock/Getty Images Plus; mariusFM77/E+; duckycards/E+; Image Source; SerAlexVi/iStock/Getty Images Plus; atoss/iStock/ Getty Images Plus; JoeGough/iStock/Getty Images Plus; Dorling Kindersley/ Getty Images Plus; etiennevoss/iStock/Getty Images Plus; Ziviani/iStock/Getty Images Plus; Kovaleva_Ka/iStock/Getty Images Plus; fcafotodigital/iStock/Getty Images Plus; nortongo/iStock/Getty Images Plus; Caziopeia/E+; lucentius/iStock/ Getty Images Plus; CQYoung/iStock/Getty Images Plus; agcuesta/iStock/Getty Images Plus; ricardoreitmeyer/iStock/Getty Images Plus; GeorgiosArt/iStock/ Getty Images Plus; vertmedia/iStock/Getty Images Plus; Dmytro/iStock/Getty Images Plus; Bozena_Fulawka/iStock/Getty Images Plus; JGI/Jamie Grill; Vinit Deekhanu/EyeEm; Jose Luis Pelaez Inc/DigitalVision; Yasser Chalid/Moment; **U4:** A. Chederros/Onoky; **U5:** Nenov/Moment; CHOI WON-SUK/Stringer/ AFP; Ralf-Finn Hestoft/Contributor/Corbis Historical; fotokon/iStock Editorial/ Getty Images Plus; AlexLMX/iStock/Getty Images Plus; Ljupco/iStock/Getty Images Plus; Lawrence Manning/Corbis; catnap72/E+; Rawf8/iStock/Getty Images Plus; **U6:** Jena Ardell/Moment; Tatiana Dyuvbanova/EyeEm; EVOK/S. Nolte; calvindexter/DigitalVision Vectors; monkeybusinessimages/iStock/Getty Images Plus; diego_cervo/iStock/Getty Images Plus; **U7:** artisteer/iStock/Getty Images Plus; by_nicholas/E+; deepblue4you/E+; macbrianmun/iStock/Getty Images Plus; dashadima/iStock/Getty Images Plus; koya79/iStock/Getty Images Plus; The Washington Post; India Herlem/EyeEm; Roman_Gorielov/iStock/ Getty Images Plus; Sheryl Saniel/EyeEm; Nnehring; Tetra Images; fullvalue/E+; **U8:** PieroAnnoni/iStock/Getty Images Plus; Laurence Mouton/PhotoAlto Agency RF Collections; Henry Georgi/Corbis; Astrakan Images/Cultura; Mike Powell/ The Image Bank/Getty Images Plus; Hirun Laowisit/EyeEm; SchulteProductions/ iStock/Getty Images Plus; skodonnell/E+; Trio Images/Photodisc; Michael Blann/Photodisc; BraunS/iStock/Getty Images Plus; Luc Beziat/Photographer's Choice/Getty Images Plus; LightFieldStudios/iStock/Getty Images Plus; bjeayes/ iStock/Getty Images Plus; Petershort/iStock/Getty Images Plus; Givaga/ iStock/Getty Images Plus; sarah5/iStock/Getty Images Plus; ddukang/iStock/ Getty Images Plus; Floortje/iStock/Getty Images Plus; technotr/E+; Keystone/ Stringer/Hulton Archive; Central Press/Stringer/Hulton Archive; Tony Duffy/ Staff/Getty Images Sport; Michael DeYoung; Matthias Tunger/The Image Bank/ Getty Images Plus; FatCamera/E+; Adie Bush/Cultura; LuckyBusiness/iStock/ Getty Images Plus; Stuart Gregory/Photodisc; Buena Vista Images/DigitalVision; svarshik/iStock Editorial/Getty Images Plus; travenian/iStock/Getty Images Plus; Jupiterimages/Stockbyte; Carol Yepes/Moment; SteveAllenPhoto/iStock Editorial/Getty Images Plus; Jung Yeon-JE/Staff/AFP; **U9:** mammuth/E+; Amaia Arozena & Gotzon Iraola/Moment; matthewleesdixon/iStock/Getty Images Plus; Knaupe/E+; spooh/E+; Serg_Velusceac/iStock/Getty Images Plus; Ralph Adolphs/500px; PhotoStock-Israel/Cultura; VargaJones/iStock/Getty Images Plus; Anna Henly/Oxford Scientific/Getty Images Plus; John W Banagan/ Lonely Planet Images/Getty Images Plus; **U10:** Barcin/iStock/Getty Images Plus; Caiaimage/Sam Edwards; BrianAJackson/iStock/Getty Images Plus; Daria Botieva/Eyeem; Richard Newstead/Moment; Aleksandrs Goldobenkovs/iStock/ Getty Images Plus; Laurence Dutton/Stone/Getty Images Plus; Phil Friar/iStock/ Getty Images Plus; Claver Carroll/Photolibrary/Getty Images Plus; Gideon Mendel/Contributor/Corbis Historical; Rich Jones Photography/Moment;

Philipp Walter/EyeEm; **U11:** XiXinXing; yacobchuk/iStock/Getty Images Plus; Eric Audras/Onoky; Damir Khabirov/iStock/Getty Images Plus; Lammeyer/iStock/ Getty Images Plus; RunPhoto/DigitalVision; energyy/iStock/Getty Images Plus; m-imagephotography/Stock/Getty Images Plus; velvelvel/iStock/Getty Images Plus; PeopleImages/E+; Guido Mieth/DigitalVision; Donald Iain Smith/Photodisc; Saturated/iStock/Getty Images Plus; The Asahi Shimbun; Janine Lamontagne/ E+; gbh007/iStock/Getty Images Plus; **U12:** william87/iStock/Getty Images Plus; m-imagephotography/iStock/Getty Images Plus; kruwt/iStock/Getty Images Plus; Image Source; MarioGuti/iStock/Getty Images Plus; Paul Biris/Moment; Solidago/ E+; gbh007/iStock/Getty Images Plus; sharply_done/iStock/Getty Images Plus; deimagine/E+; MStudioImages/E+.

Cover photographs by: Antonio Ferreira Silva/EyeEm/Getty Images; PeopleImages/iStock/Getty Images Plus/Getty Images

The following image is sourced from other source/library:

SafeWander for the image in Unit 7. Copyright © 2019 SafeWander. Reproduced with kind permission.

Illustrations

Dusan Lakicevic (Beehive Illustration) pp. 4, 37, 38, 70; Emma Nyari (Beehive Illustration) pp. 5, 19, 66, 91, 112; Mark Ruffle pp. 7, 25; Lisa Reed (The Bright Agency) pp. 13, 20, 52, 73, 108; Tom Heard (The Bright Agency) pp. 16, 30, 61, 62, 82, 101, 111; Michael McCabe (Beehive Illustration) pp. 18, 29, 42, 88; Adam Linley (Beehive Illustration) pp. 21, 54, 64, 92; Martin Sanders (Beehive Illustration) pp. 93, 114;

Grammar Rap video stills: Silversun Media Group.

Full video acknowledgements can be found in the online Teacher`s Resources.

Audio Production: Leon Chambers.

CONTENTS

WELCOME

A ALL ABOUT ME
Personal information

1 Match the sentences and the replies.

1 What's your name? ☐
2 How old are you? ☐
3 Where are you from? ☐
4 Hi, I'm Ava. ☐
5 This is my friend George. ☐
6 Nice to meet you. ☐

a I'm 14.
b Hi, Ava, I'm Laura.
c Hi, George. Nice to meet you.
d Nice to meet you, too.
e My name's Saul.
f I'm from Boston in the US.

2 Write <u>your</u> answers to questions 1–3 in Exercise 1.

1 _____
_____
2 _____
_____
3 _____
_____

Nationalities and *be*

3 Find 10 more countries in the wordsearch.

T	C	O	L	O	M	B	I	A	O	N
K	J	C	M	Z	F	I	U	A	R	E
A	R	G	E	N	T	I	N	A	Y	T
U	T	T	X	T	Y	U	O	U	E	H
S	C	U	I	K	L	U	Y	W	A	E
T	H	R	C	O	L	U	M	B	I	R
R	I	K	O	A	Y	I	E	J	S	L
A	N	E	X	P	L	P	W	N	S	A
L	A	Y	I	P	A	I	N	F	U	N
I	P	N	W	U	T	T	M	P	R	D
A	B	R	A	Z	I	L	D	M	O	S
P	A	L	R	M	U	I	G	L	E	B

4 Complete with the verb *to be*.

0 It _____'s_____ a Ferrari.
1 They _____ from Moscow.
2 I _____ (not) from London.
3 _____ Lena from New York?
4 _____ you from São Paulo?
5 We _____ (not) from Barcelona.
6 Daan _____ from a small town near Amsterdam.
7 My dad _____ (not) from China.

5 Match the sentences 0–7 in Exercise 4 with a–h.

a We're from Madrid. ☐
b They're Russian. ☐
c He's Dutch. ☐
d But he is Chinese. ☐
e Yes, I'm Brazilian. ☐
f It's an Italian car. ☐
g I'm from Liverpool. ☐
h Yes, she's American. ☐

6 Complete the sentences with the nationality.

0 Logan is from the US. He's ____*American*____ .
1 Juana's from Mexico. She's _____ .
2 Henry's from the UK. He's _____ .
3 Isabella's from Spain. She's _____ .
4 Adem and Adile are from Turkey. They're _____ .
5 My best friend's from Belgium. She's _____ .
6 Fang and Jia are from China. They're _____ .
7 Anatoly's from Russia. He's _____ .
8 My mum's from Argentina. She's _____ .

Names and addresses

7 🔊 W.01 Listen to the phone conversation. Who is the girl calling? Tick (✓) the box.

A ☐

B ☐

C ☐

8 🔊 **W.01** Listen again and complete the form.

Barney's

Day [1] _____

Time [2] _____

Table for [3] _____ **people**

Name [4] _____

Phone number
[5] _____

9 🔊 **W.01** Put the dialogue in order. Listen again and check.

☐ **Man** Thank you, Emma. Collins ... Is that
C – O – L – L – I – N – S?

☐ **Man** And can you give me a contact phone number, please?

☐ **Man** How many is the table for?

`1` **Man** Hello, Barney's Pizza Kitchen.

☐ **Man** Great, Emma. See you all on Saturday.

☐ **Man** Just a moment ... Let me check our reservation book. Yes, that's OK. What time?

☐ **Man** OK. So that's a table for ten at 8 pm on Saturday. Can I take your name?

☐ **Girl** There are ten of us. It's for a birthday.

☐ **Girl** Sure, it's Emma Collins.

☐ **Girl** Yes, it's 0796353291.

☐ **Girl** Yes, that's right.

☐ **Girl** Hi, I'd like to book a table for Saturday evening.

☐ **Girl** 8 o'clock, please.

SUMMING UP

10 **Complete the text with the verb *be* and the nationalities.**

I really love basketball! This is my dream team with my favourite players from all over the world!
Fernandez and Diaz [1] _____
from Rio de Janeiro. They [2] _____
[3] _____ .
Cruz [4] _____ from Madrid.
He [5] _____ [6] _____ .
Janssens [7] _____ [8] _____ .
He [9] _____ from Brussels.
Campbell and Abanda [10] _____
[11] _____ . Campbell
[12] _____ from London and Abanda
[13] _____ from Manchester.
The other players [14] _____
[15] _____ . They [16] _____
from lots of different cities in the US.

B WHAT'S THAT?
Things in the classroom and prepositions of place

1 Find and ⟨circle⟩ 12 classroom items in the word snake.

doorboardrulerfloorcdnotebookwindowpenbookchairpencildesk

2 Look at the picture. Complete the sentences with the classroom objects in the list.

board | chair | notebook | pen | ruler | teacher

1 The _____ is under the chair.

2 The _____ is behind the teacher's desk.

3 The _____ is on the desk.

4 The _____ is in front of the board.

5 The _____ is between the door and the window.

6 The _____ is on a book.

Classroom language

3 Put the words in order to make sentences and questions.

1 I / a / Can / question /ask

_____

2 again / Can / say / that / you

_____

3 page / your / Open / at / 10 / books

_____

4 don't / I / know

_____

5 I / understand / don't

_____

6 mean / word / does / What / this

_____

7 that / do / word / spell / you / How

_____

8 English / How / say / *amanhã* / in / do / you

_____

9 If / hand / your / know / up / answer / put / you / the

_____

Object pronouns

4 Complete the table.

__I__	0 __me__
you	1 _____
he	2 _____
she	3 _____
it	4 _____
we	5 _____
they	6 _____

5 Circle the correct words.

0 Erin's my best friend. I tell *she /* *her* everything.

1 *They / Them* don't speak English. That's why you don't understand *they / them*.

2 *I / Me* love this T-shirt. Buy it for *I / me*, please.

3 Turn the music up. *We / Us* can't hear it.

4 Robbie's got a problem and *I / me* can't help *he / him*.

5 Our gran gives *we / us* great presents on our birthdays.

6 Complete the sentences with the missing object pronouns.

0 I want my sandwich! Give it to ____me____ .

1 That's Mr O'Brian. Say hello to _____ .

2 Mum wants some help. Can you help _____ ?

3 I love _____ . You're my best friend.

4 We really want to go to the show. Can you buy _____ some tickets?

5 The children are very noisy. Tell _____ to be quiet, please.

this, that, these, those

7 Circle the correct words.

1 *This / These* homework is very difficult.

2 *That / Those* shoes are really nice.

3 *That / These* house is really old.

4 *These / This* books aren't very interesting.

8 Complete the sentences with *this, that, these* or *those*.

1 Can you pass me _____ magazines next to you, please?

2 Is _____ my phone in your hand?

3 _____ pencil is broken. Can you give me another one?

4 _____ sandwiches are really nice! Thanks!

SUMMING UP

9 W.02 Complete the dialogue with the words in the list. Then listen and check.

```
ask | know | notebook | pen
put | say | spell | that | this
```

Roberto Excuse me, Miss Baker, can I
⁰ _____ask_____ you a question?

Miss Baker Of course you can, Roberto.

Roberto How do you ¹_____ 'pizza' in English?

Miss Baker Ahmed. Can you help?

Ahmed Sorry. I don't ²_____ .

Miss Baker Can anyone help Roberto?
³_____ your hands up if you know the answer. Yes, Kim.

Kim It's easy. It's 'pizza'.

Roberto How do you ⁴_____ that?

Kim P–I–Z–Z–A, it's the same as in Italian!

Roberto OK, let me write that in my
⁵_____ . Is ⁶_____ your ⁷_____ ? Can I borrow it?

Kim No, ⁸_____'s your pen. You don't need to ask.

C ABOUT TIME
Days and dates

1 Sort the words into three different groups.
There are four words in each group.

> fourteenth | Friday | July | March
> Monday | October | Saturday | second
> September | Sunday | tenth | third

_____	_____	_____
_____	_____	_____
_____	_____	_____
_____	_____	_____

2 Write the next word in each sequence.

1 February, April, June, _____
2 Friday, Thursday, Wednesday, _____
3 first, third, sixth, _____
4 1st, 10th, 19th, _____
5 April, August, December, _____
6 4th, 8th, 12th, _____
7 Monday, Wednesday, Friday, _____
8 December, November, October, _____

3 Write the numbers in words.

1 1st _____
2 4th _____
3 8th _____
4 11th _____
5 12th _____
6 15th _____
7 20th _____
8 22nd _____
9 25th _____
10 29th _____
11 30th _____
12 31st _____

4 Answer the questions.

When is …
1 your birthday?
_____
2 your country's national day?
_____
3 your best friend's birthday?
_____
4 the first day of your next school holiday?
_____

My day

5 Write the times.

0 It's ___4 o'clock___ .   3 It's _____ .

1 It's _____ .   4 It's _____ .

2 It's _____ .   5 It's _____ .

6 Put the events in order from morning to night.

☐ I have lunch at quarter past one.
☐ I go to bed at twenty past eight.
☐ I go to school at seven o'clock.
☐ I have dinner at half past six in the evening.
☐ I have breakfast at quarter past six.
☐ I get home at half past one.
1 I get up at six o'clock.
☐ I do my homework at quarter to two.

7 Now write about your day.

1 _I get up at …_ _____
2 _____
3 _____
4 _____
5 _____
6 _____
7 _____
8 _____

SUMMING UP

8 🔊 W.03 **Listen and write the times that David does the following things.**

1 get up on Tuesday morning

_____

2 arrive at school

_____

3 get home after school

_____

4 go to bed

_____

5 get up on Sunday morning

_____

9 🔊 W.03 **Complete the dialogue with David's answers (a–f). Then listen and check.**

Orla What time do you get up, David?

David ⁰ $\boxed{d}$

Orla Half past six in the morning! That's early. Why?

David ¹ ☐

Orla Oh. And what time does it finish?

David ² ☐

Orla What do you do after lunch?

David ³ ☐

Orla So, do you love getting up late at the weekend?

David ⁴ ☐

Orla What! Six o'clock??!!

David ⁵ ☐

a I do homework and watch TV. Sometimes I play football or basketball. Then it's dinner and I go to bed at nine o'clock.

b Well, my school starts at eight o'clock, so I get there at ten to eight.

c Yes. Six o'clock. I have early morning swimming lessons.

d From Monday to Friday I get up at half past six.

e Twenty past one, so I get home at ten to two for lunch.

f No, I don't. On Saturdays and Sundays I get up at 6 o'clock.

D MY THINGS
My possessions

1 **Complete the word puzzle and find the name of Joe's pet.**

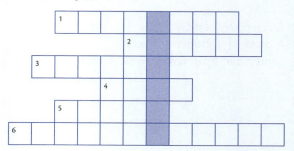

have got

2 **Complete the sentences about Joe with *has* or *hasn't*.**

1 Joe _____ got a skateboard.

2 Joe _____ got a camera.

3 Joe _____ got a phone.

4 Joe _____ got a bike.

5 Joe _____ got a dog.

6 Joe _____ got a tennis racket.

3 Match the questions (1–6) with the answers (a–f).

1 Have you got a pet? ☐

2 Has Johnny got a cat? ☐

3 Have all your friends got smartphones? ☐

4 Has your brother got a bike? ☐

5 Have you got a skateboard? ☐

6 Has Suzie got a brother? ☐

a Yes, they have.

b Yes, I've got a goldfish.

c No, he hasn't.

d No, she hasn't, but she's got a sister.

e No, I haven't.

f Yes, he has. It's called Mickey.

4 (Circle) the correct words.

1 I *have / has* got three brothers.

2 We *haven't / hasn't* got a garden.

3 Sienna *has / have* got a new friend.

4 They *haven't / hasn't* got any pets.

5 James *haven't / hasn't* got homework tonight.

6 I *haven't / hasn't* got a pen. *Have / Has* you got one?

5 Complete the dialogue with *have, has, haven't* or *hasn't*.

Megan ¹_____ you got a laptop, Nick?

Nick No, I ²_____ , but I'd love one.

Megan What about your brother? ³_____ he got one?

Nick Yes, he ⁴_____ and he ⁵_____ got a tablet too.

Megan That's not fair.

Nick He's older than me. My sister ⁶_____ got one, but she's only three.

Megan ⁷_____ your parents got a digital camera?

Nick Yes, they ⁸_____ . I use it sometimes.

6 Write sentences.

1 Two things you have got and two things you haven't got.

_____

_____

_____

_____

2 Two things your best friend has got and two things he/she hasn't got.

_____

_____

_____

_____

I like and *I'd like*

7 (Circle) the correct words.

1 A What's your favourite colour?

B I *like / 'd like* blue best.

2 A Can I help you?

B Yes, I *like / 'd like* an ice cream, please.

3 A What do you want to do?

B I *like / 'd like* to play computer games.

4 A Do you want apple or orange juice?

B I *like / 'd like* apple juice, please.

5 A Who's the best teacher at your school?

B I *like / 'd like* Miss Dawes. She's really nice.

6 A Which day of the week do you like the most?

B I *like / 'd like* Fridays.

7 A Do you want anything to eat?

B I *like / 'd like* some chicken soup, please.

8 A What do you do in your free time?

B I *like / 'd like* swimming and playing volleyball.

SUMMING UP

8 🔊 **W.04** Write questions for the answers. Then listen and check.

1 A _____ ?

B Yes, I'd love a <u>rabbit or cat</u>.

2 A _____ ? (football)

B No, I don't. I don't like <u>any sports</u>.

3 A _____ ?

B Yes, I am. Very. I'd love <u>a sandwich</u>, please.

4 A _____ ?

B Yes, I do. Especially <u>bananas and apples</u>.

5 A _____ ?

B Yes, I have. I've got <u>a brother and two sisters</u>.

6 A _____ ?

B No, Rosie hasn't got <u>a bird</u>, but I think she's got some goldfish.

7 A _____ ?

B Yes, please. I'd love <u>a glass of water</u>. I'm really thirsty.

8 A _____ ?

B No, we haven't got <u>a car</u>, but we've all got bikes.

9 A _____ ?

B Yes, I love <u>cats</u>. We've got two.

10 A _____ ?

B No, I haven't got <u>a tablet</u>, but I've got a phone.

1 HAVING A GOOD TIME

Grammar rap!
▶ 02

GRAMMAR
Present simple

→ SB p.14

1 ⭐☆☆ (Circle) the correct words.

0 My mum *go* /*goes* to work by car.

1 He *think* / *thinks* I'm crazy.

2 Gemma *look* / *looks* quite angry.

3 Dad *wash* / *washes* his car every Sunday.

4 I *doesn't* / *don't* feel very good.

5 Simon *doesn't* / *don't* want to have a shower now.

6 We *doesn't* / *don't* live very close to our school.

2 ⭐⭐☆ Rewrite the sentences. Make the positive sentences negative. Make the negative sentences positive.

0 Stephanie doesn't watch a lot of TV.

Stephanie watches a lot of TV.

1 I like dancing.

_____

2 Ken plays the guitar in a band.

_____

3 Kelly doesn't miss her family a lot.

_____

4 My parents work at the weekend.

_____

3 ⭐⭐☆ Make questions in the present simple.

0 where / you / live?

Where do you live?

1 you / speak / French?

_____

2 when / school / start / in the morning?

_____

3 your teacher / give you / lots of homework?

_____

4 what / music / you / like?

_____

5 you / play / instrument?

_____

4 ⭐⭐☆ Match the questions in Exercise 3 with the answers (a–f). Write 1–5.

a At 8 o'clock. ☐

b Yes, I do. The piano. ☐

c Just outside London. [0]

d Yes, she does. Every day. ☐

e No, I don't. ☐

f I don't really like music. ☐

5 ⭐⭐⭐ Write answers to the questions in Exercise 3 so they are true for you.

0 _____

1 _____

2 _____

3 _____

4 _____

5 _____

6 ⭐⭐⭐ Read about Oliver's hobby. Complete the text with the correct form of the words in the list.

~~not collect~~ | not do | not play | not think | phone
say | see | stand | tell | try | turn | write

My friend Oliver has a really unusual hobby.
He ⁰ _____*doesn't collect*_____ football cards and
he ¹_____ the piano. No, these
are normal hobbies. Oliver's hobby is really
strange. His hobby is being on TV. Every time he
² _____ a TV cameraman and
presenter in town he ³_____
behind the presenter and ⁴_____
to appear on TV.
Then he ⁵_____ me and
⁶ _____ me to watch the news
on TV. So I ⁷_____ on the TV
and there he is. He ⁸_____
anything silly. He's just there smiling. Then he
⁹ _____ about it on his blog.
He ¹⁰_____ he's famous.
I ¹¹_____ he's famous, just
a bit crazy!

PRONUNCIATION
Plurals and third person verb endings: /s/, /z/
or /ɪz/ Go to page 118. 🎧

like + -ing

 SB p.17

7 ★★☆ **Complete the sentences with the verbs in the list.**

| chat | do | get | go | help | read | ~~take~~ | tidy |

Best and worst things to do on a Saturday morning.

0 I love *taking* my dog for a walk.
1 I enjoy _____ Dad make breakfast.
2 I like _____ for a bike ride with my friends.
3 I love _____ a book in bed.
4 I enjoy _____ with my friends on social media.
5 I hate _____ my homework.
6 I can't stand _____ up my bedroom.
7 I hate _____ out of bed before midday.

8 ★★★ **What about you? What do you like (and hate) doing on Saturday mornings? Complete the sentences so they are true for you.**

1 I love _____
2 I enjoy _____
3 I like _____
4 I hate _____
5 I can't stand _____

Adverbs of frequency

 SB p.17

9 ★☆☆ **Match the word parts to make adverbs of frequency. Then write them in the correct place.**

occasion	ten		100%	*always*
ne	~~ways~~		↑	_____
rare	times		↑	_____
some	ally		↑	_____
a~~l~~	ly		↑	_____
usu	ally		↑	_____
of	ver		0%	_____

10 ★★☆ **Rewrite the sentences with the adverb of frequency in the correct place.**

0 I play computer games after dinner. (usually)
I usually play computer games after dinner.

1 You are happy. (always)
_____

2 My best friend stays with us in the holidays. (often)
_____

3 My mum and dad go out for a meal. (occasionally)
_____

4 My sister is nice to me. (rarely)
_____

5 My friends and I go to the cinema on a Saturday morning. (sometimes)
_____

6 You are sad. (never)
_____

11 ★★★ **Answer the questions so they are true for you.**

1 What do you always do at the weekend?
_____

2 What do you rarely do after school?
_____

3 What do you usually do when you're bored?
_____

4 What do you sometimes do in the evening?
_____

5 What do you never do on a Monday?
_____

6 What do you often do when you're happy?
_____

GET IT RIGHT!

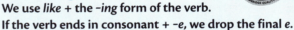

like + -ing

We use *like* + the *-ing* form of the verb.
If the verb ends in consonant + *-e*, we drop the final *e*.

✓ live – living   ✗ live – ~~liveing~~

If a <u>short</u> verb ends in consonant + vowel + consonant, we double the final consonant before adding the *-ing*.

✓ swim – swi**mming**   ✗ swim – ~~swiming~~

With verbs with two or more syllables, we do not usually double the final consonant.

✓ listen – listen**ing**   ✗ listen – ~~listenning~~

Correct the *-ing* forms.

1 writting _____
2 comming _____
3 studing _____
4 waitting _____
5 chating _____
6 useing _____
7 listenning _____
8 planing _____
9 rainning _____
10 geting _____

𝐀𝐳 VOCABULARY
Hobbies

⟶ SB p.14

1 ★☆☆ **Read the speech bubbles. Choose a word from each list and write the hobbies.**

> be | collect | keep | play | take | ~~write~~

> ~~a blog~~ | an instrument | a pet
> in a club | photos | things

0 *It's about my life. It's about my friends and my family. It's about the things I enjoy doing (and some of the things I don't enjoy). It's about everything and anything. Read it!*

_____ write a blog _____

1 *I'm in a band. I'm the guitarist.
I play for about two hours every day.*

_____

2 *We meet every Friday from 7 pm to 9 pm. We learn how to do things like how to play new games or how to cook. It's really good fun.*

_____

3 *I've got about 15 mugs now. I've got big ones, medium-sized ones and small ones. Every time I visit a new city I always buy one.*

_____

4 *It's quite hard work. Every morning I wake up early to take him for a walk and then when I get home from school I take him for another walk.*

_____

5 *These are from my last holidays. We were in Corfu. It was really great. I spent hours with my camera.*

_____

2 ★★☆ **Write four words that go with each verb in the boxes.**

	a team	
an orchestra	**be in**	a club
	a band	

	collect	

	write	

	play	

3 ★★★ **Use your ideas in Exercise 2 to write four sentences that are true for you.**

0 *I'm in the school football team.* _____
1 _____
2 _____
3 _____
4 _____

WordWise: Collocations with *have*

⟶ SB p.15

4 ★★☆ **Complete the sentences with the words in the list.**

> dinner | fun | problem | rest | ~~shower~~ | time

0 Do you usually have a _shower_ when you wake up or before you go to bed?
1 Who do you always ask for help when you have a _____ with your homework?
2 Do you always have a _____ when you feel tired?
3 What time does your family usually have _____ ?
4 Do you always have a good _____ when you're on holiday?
5 What do you do to have _____ at the weekend?

5 ★★★ **Write answers to the questions in Exercise 4 so they are true for you.**

0 _____
1 _____
2 _____
3 _____
4 _____
5 _____

REFERENCE

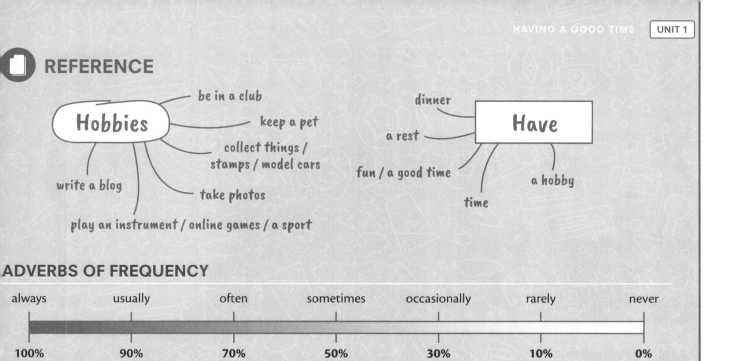

Hobbies
- be in a club
- keep a pet
- collect things / stamps / model cars
- take photos
- play an instrument / online games / a sport
- write a blog

Have
- dinner
- a rest
- fun / a good time
- time
- a hobby

ADVERBS OF FREQUENCY

always	usually	often	sometimes	occasionally	rarely	never
100%	90%	70%	50%	30%	10%	0%

VOCABULARY *EXTRA*

1 Complete the hobbies with the words in the list.

> books | cinema | exercise | ~~language~~ | pictures | videos

0 learn a *language*

1 draw _____

2 record _____

3 read _____

4 go to the _____

5 do _____

2 Do you like the hobbies in Exercise 1? Write them in order of preference for you.

1 _____   3 _____   5 _____
2 _____   4 _____   6 _____

UNUSUAL HOBBIES

1 _____

2 _____

3 _____

Gina Jones and her sister Karen have the same hobby. They both love photography. In fact, they are both in a photography club. But they don't take photographs of their friends or the interesting places they go to. They take photographs of other people taking photographs! They have a big collection – more than 2,000. They write a blog about their hobby and you can see all their photos on it. The sisters don't know the people in their photos. They are just people they see in the street. But they always ask them if they can use the photos for their blog. Most people say 'yes'.

58-year-old **Dan Baker** loves roller coasters. Every Saturday he visits the Alton Towers theme park and spends all day on them. Luckily, he lives very near to it. Some days he has more than 50 rides. His favourites are Nemesis and Th13teen. He doesn't take his wife with him – she hates roller coasters – but he often takes his grandchildren or brother. He also collects postcards of roller coasters. Every holiday he travels to theme parks in different countries: Six Flags in Mexico, PortAventura in Spain and Everland in South Korea. But Dan wants more. He wants to ride every roller coaster in the world.

Adam Roberts is a bit different from a lot of other teenagers. He likes animals. That's nothing strange. Many people his age like animals. He also keeps animals as pets. There's nothing unusual about that, either. But do most teens keep spiders, lizards and snakes? Adam does. He has a spider from Brazil, a lizard from Australia and a snake from South Africa. He buys them from his local pet shop. He spends all his pocket money on his pets, and he also spends a lot of his time looking after them. Adam knows what he wants to do when he is older. He wants to work in the insect house at a zoo.

READING

1 Read the text quickly. Write the names under the pictures.

2 Complete the sentences with a name: Gina, Dan or Adam.

   0 _Dan_ enjoys going to theme parks.
   1 _____ spends all his/her money on one hobby.
   2 _____ is married.
   3 _____'s sister has the same hobby.
   4 _____ knows where he/she wants to work.
   5 _____ travels the world for this hobby.
   6 _____ uses the Internet for this hobby.

3 **CRITICAL THINKING** Which person in Exercise 1 says these things about their hobby?

   1 *I can forget all my problems and have fun!* _____

   2 *I learn a lot. I learn all about their food, where they live and their habits.* _____

   3 *It's a great way to go out and meet new people.* _____

4 **Write the names of two of your hobbies. Then write why they are good for you.**

   Dancing: I make new friends at my dance class and I learn how to dance. It's fun, too.

   1 _____
   2 _____

Routines

1 **INPUT** **Read about Amy's hobby. Tick (✓) the photo that matches her blog.**

 **1**

 **2**

 **3**

⌂ **HOME**   ⓘ **ABOUT**   ▤ **NEWS**   ✉ **CONTACT**

Every weekend, I go to a theatre group and I love it! Acting isn't a very unusual hobby, but my group is special. We only do mime, so we never talk in our shows. Instead, we move, we dance and we use music to tell a story. I've got lots of friends in the group and we always have fun – but when we're on stage, we don't speak.

The mime group usually meets on Saturday mornings, but before a show, we meet three times a week to practise.

Mime is special because you learn to communicate without speaking. Some of my friends don't like speaking in front of big groups of people, but they're good at mime.

2 **Complete the sentences with *and, but, to* or *so*.**

1 Amy and her friends do mime _____ they really enjoy it.

2 They don't speak, _____ they don't need to learn any words.

3 They need to practise a lot _____ be ready for a show.

4 Learning to do mime is hard work, _____ it's fun.

3 **ANALYSE** **Tick (✓) the information Amy includes in her blog.**

1 The name of the hobby. ☐

2 How often she does her hobby. ☐

3 The names of the people in her group. ☐

4 The activities they do. ☐

5 Why she likes her hobby. ☐

6 The things she doesn't like. ☐

4 **PLAN** **Answer the questions so they are true for you.**

1 What is your hobby?
_____

2 How often do you do it?
_____

3 Where do you do it?
_____

4 Who do you do it with?
_____

5 What do you like about it?
_____

6 What do you not like about it?
_____

5 **Write sentences using your answers from Exercise 4. Try to use *and, but, to* and *so* to connect some of your ideas.**
_____
_____
_____
_____

✏ **WRITING TIP: Connectors**

We use *but, and, to* and *so* to connect two ideas in a sentence.

- We use *but* to express a contrast.
  *It's difficult, **but** it's fun.*
- We use *and* to add information.
  *I like dancing **and** singing.*
- We use *to* to express an objective.
  *We go to school **to** learn.*
- We use *so* to express a consequence.
  *He does a lot of sport, **so** he gets hungry.*

6 **PRODUCE** **Write a short paragraph about your hobby (about 100–120 words). Include the sentences in Exercise 5.**

🎧 LISTENING

1 🔊 1.03 **Listen to the conversations. Choose the correct answer A, B or C.**

Conversation 1

1 What is Alice's hobby?

  A cooking

  B dancing

  C taking photos

Conversation 2

2 What's the problem?

  A Leo can't find his things.

  B Lily doesn't like judo.

  C Lily isn't ready.

Conversation 3

3 What does Eva want to do?

  A keep a pet

  B start a new hobby

  C paint a picture of Tom

DIALOGUE

2 🔊 1.04 **Put the words in order to make sentences. Then listen and check.**

1 but / OK, / look / out / !

_____

2 near / do / that / Don't / plates / those / !

_____

3 pictures / on / wall / Be / of / the / careful / the / !

_____

4 What / up / to, / you / are / Tom / ?

_____

3 **Write a short conversation for each picture. Use some of the expressions in Exercise 2.**

1 _____

_____

_____

_____

2 _____

_____

_____

_____

PHRASES FOR FLUENCY → SB p.18

4 **Match the phrases (1–6) with their meanings (a–f).**

1 up to ☐		**a** correct
2 come on ☐		**b** doing
3 look out ☐		**c** great
4 that's right ☐		**d** let's go
5 hurry up ☐		**e** be careful
6 cool ☐		**f** be quick

5 🔊 1.05 **Complete the conversations with the phrases 1–6 from Exercise 4. Then listen and check.**

Conversation 1

Oscar What are you ⁰_____ *up to* _____?

Shona I'm just doing a bit of drawing.

Oscar Let's have a look.

Shona Here. What do you think?

Oscar Is it a picture of Jen?

Shona ¹_____ . What do you think?

Oscar ²_____ ! It's really good.

Conversation 2

Lucy ³_____ , Joel.

Joel OK, OK. I'm coming. Just give me a minute.

Lucy ⁴_____ , Joel. Run.

Joel I am running!

Lucy ⁵_____ . Don't run into the door. Too late!

Joel Ow! That hurts.

A2 Key for Schools

📖 READING AND WRITING
Part 1: 3-option multiple choice

1 For each question, choose the correct answer.

1

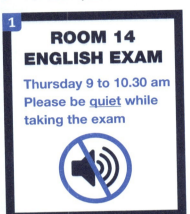

ROOM 14 ENGLISH EXAM

Thursday 9 to 10.30 am
Please be <u>quiet</u> while taking the exam

A Be careful in this classroom.
B Don't use this classroom.
C Don't talk in this classroom.

4

15:32

Chloe,
I'm bored!
It's a nice day.
What are you up to?
Do you want to come to the park with me and Ellen?
Jade

Why is Jade writing to Chloe?

A Jade is contacting Chloe to change their plans.
B Jade is inviting Chloe to go out with her and Ellen.
C Jade is asking Chloe if she has met Ellen before.

2

14:10

Hi Damon,
We haven't got basketball practice after school today. The coach's sick. The next practice is on Friday at 4 pm.
See you then,
Freddie

A Basketball practice starts at 4 pm today.
B Basketball practice is on a different day this week.
C There are two basketball practices this week.

5

CAUTION!

WILD ANIMALS IN THIS AREA

Drive carefully, especially after dark

A Don't drive at night in this area.
B Cars cannot drive on this road.
C Look out for wild animals in this area.

3

Do you enjoy **reading?**

Then come to Tuesday's Book Club!
School library
12–1 pm

A There's a reading group on Tuesdays.
B The library isn't open on Tuesdays at noon.
C There's a book club on Tuesday mornings.

6

16:07

Hi Luis,
I don't understand the homework.
Have you got time to help me?
I can call you in 10 minutes.
Ed

A Ed needs the answers to the homework.
B Ed wants Luis to call him.
C Ed has got a problem.

EXAM GUIDE: READING AND WRITING PART 1

In A2 Key for Schools Reading and Writing Part 1, there are six short texts and you choose the option with the correct meaning. The texts are usually notices, signs, emails or text messages. There are three options and you choose one.

- Read the text. Don't worry if you don't understand all the words. Focus on general understanding.
- Read the three options A, B and C.
- Read the text again and eliminate any of the options you are sure are wrong.
- Before you choose, compare the other options with the text again.
- Make your final choice.

2 SPENDING MONEY

Grammar rap! ▶ 05

GRAMMAR
Present continuous
→ SB p.22

1 ★☆☆ **Complete the sentences with the names.**

Mason

Clare | Josh

Dylan

Sophie | Stella

0 _Sophie_ and _Stella_ are laughing about some funny hats.

1 _____ is looking at the bike prices.

2 _____ is buying a digital camera.

3 _____ is trying on a T-shirt.

2 ★★☆ **Complete the sentences. Use the present continuous of the verbs in brackets.**

0 Felix _____ _isn't studying_ _____ (not study) English.
He _____ _'s studying_ _____ (study) Maths.

1 We _____ (take) the bus to school. We _____ (not walk).

2 Riley and Amelie _____ (not have) fun. They _____ (work) on a project.

3 I _____ (try) to finish my homework. I _____ (not take) a break.

4 We _____ (play) computer games. We _____ (not listening) to music.

5 Abigail _____ (not have) lunch. She _____ (help) her dad.

3 ★★☆ **Match the questions with the answers.**

0 Are you having fun? | d

1 Is Joseph in the garden? | ☐

2 What are you studying? | ☐

3 Are they playing basketball? | ☐

4 Am I talking too loudly? | ☐

5 Is he studying for the test? | ☐

a Yes, he is. He's cutting the grass.

b No, they're watching a film.

c No, don't worry. It's OK.

d No, I'm not. I've got a lot of work to do for school.

e Yes, he is. He's in his room.

f French. I'm trying to remember some new words.

4 ★★★ **Complete the conversation. Use the correct form of the verbs in the list.**

> cry | ~~do~~ | get | laugh (x2)
> not sit | run | sit | try (x2)

Libby Look at that man over there! What ⁰_is he doing_ ?

Gabriel Hmm. I think he ¹_____ to climb the tree.

Libby Oh yes, there's a cat up there. Look. It ²_____ high up in the tree.

Gabriel Oh yes. Poor cat. What's that strange noise? ³_____ it _____ ?

Libby Yeah, it's scared. Look. The man ⁴_____ closer to the cat.

Gabriel But it's scared of the man, too.

Libby Oh, no. It ⁵_____ to jump down. I just hope …

Gabriel There it goes. It's down.

Libby Wow. Look how fast it ⁶_____ now.

Gabriel Well, I guess it's happy it ⁷_____ in the tree anymore.

Libby Hey, look at those people over there. They ⁸_____ , so the cat must be OK.

Gabriel That's right. And you ⁹_____ too now!

PRONUNCIATION
Contractions Go to page 118.

Verbs of perception

→ SB p.23

5 ★★☆ **Look at the conversations. Choose the correct options.**

0 A What do you think of this song?
 B It (sounds) / is sounding really cool.

1 A What are you thinking about?
 B My homework. It *looks* / *is looking* difficult.

2 A How do you like this T-shirt?
 B It *doesn't look* / *is not looking* very nice.

3 A Would you like some lunch?
 B Yes, please. It *smells* / *is smelling* nice.

4 A Do you like the soup?
 B Yes, it *tastes* / *is tasting* wonderful.

5 A Do you like this tattoo?
 B To be honest, I think it *looks* / *is looking* awful.

6 ★★★ **Look at the examples. Write four sentences that are true for you. Use** *look, sound, smell* **and** *taste* **and adjectives such as** *interesting, boring, cool, awful, wonderful* **and** *exciting.*

Raindrops on the window sound relaxing.
Lemon ice cream with chocolate chips tastes awful.

1 _____
2 _____
3 _____
4 _____

Present simple vs. present continuous

→ SB p.25

7 ★☆☆ **Match the pictures with the sentences.**

0 She studies English every day. d
1 She teaches Maths. ☐
2 She is studying for her English test. ☐
3 She is teaching Maths. ☐

8 ★★★ **Complete the email. Use the present continuous or the present simple of the verbs in brackets.**

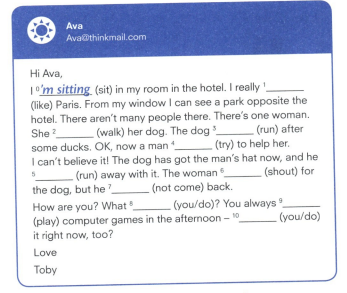

Ava
Ava@thinkmail.com

Hi Ava,
I ⁰*'m sitting* (sit) in my room in the hotel. I really ¹_____ (like) Paris. From my window I can see a park opposite the hotel. There aren't many people there. There's one woman. She ²_____ (walk) her dog. The dog ³_____ (run) after some ducks. OK, now a man ⁴_____ (try) to help her. I can't believe it! The dog has got the man's hat now, and he ⁵_____ (run) away with it. The woman ⁶_____ (shout) for the dog, but he ⁷_____ (not come) back.
How are you? What ⁸_____ (you/do)? You always ⁹_____ (play) computer games in the afternoon – ¹⁰_____ (you/do) it right now, too?
Love
Toby

GET IT RIGHT!

Present simple vs. present continuous

Present simple: for things that happen regularly or that are always true.

✓ I never **shop** online

✗ I ~~am never shopping~~ online.

Present continuous: for things that are happening at or around the time of speaking.

✓ We're **studying** English today.

✗ ~~We study English today.~~

Remember: we don't usually use verbs that describe emotions or the way we think in the present continuous (e.g. *think* / *need* / *like*, **etc.).**

✓ I **think** it's a good idea.

✗ ~~I'm thinking it's a good idea.~~

(Circle) the correct options.

BIKE FOR SALE!

I ¹*sell* / *am selling* my bike. It's five years old, but it ²*is looking* / *looks* new. I ³*like* / *am liking* this bike very much, but I ⁴*want* / *am wanting* to sell it because it's too small for me. My name is Leon, and I ⁵*am coming* / *come* to school on my bike every day. I can show it to you. This week I ⁶*am studying* / *study* in room 3C. You can find me there!

VOCABULARY
Shops

→ SB p.22

1 ★☆☆ **Write the names of the shops under the objects.**

0 _chemist's_

3 _____

1 _____

4 _____

2 _____

5 _____

2 ★★☆ **Complete the conversation with the shops from Exercise 1.**

Mollie So, here's the shopping list.

Liam OK, which shops do we need to go to?

Mollie The ⁰_supermarket_ . We need to buy food for the party.

Liam Let's go there last. We don't want to carry all that shopping round with us!

Mollie Yes, you're right. What else do we need?

Liam Well, I need some new football shorts. The ¹_____ isn't far. Let's go there first.

Mollie No, no, no. I want to get a new dress for the party. We can start at the ²_____ .

Liam OK, but don't forget Mum's birthday. We are thinking of getting her a book, right?

Mollie Yes, I think so. Let's go to the ³_____ .

Liam Yes, we're sure to find something good to read there.

Mollie Listen. I've got an idea! There's a new ⁴_____ in Silver Street. We can sit down, have a nice hot drink and decide which shops to go to.

Liam Good plan!

3 ★★★ **Look at the sentences. Rewrite them so they are true for you.**

1 There's a chemist's near our house, but we only go there when we need medicines.

_____

2 I never go to a clothes shop. I buy all my clothes online.

_____

3 There's a good mobile phone shop in the town centre. I often go there.

_____

Clothes

→ SB p.24

4 ★★☆ **Write the words.**

0 btle   _belt_   **5** osetsrur _____

1 tobos _____   **6** hoses _____

2 sreds _____   **7** rtossh _____

3 keajct _____   **8** hirst _____

4 erpumj _____   **9** restnair _____

5 ★★☆ **Complete the text with words from Exercise 4.**

Sebastian likes black. His ⁰_trousers_ and his ¹_____ are black, his ²_____ and his ³_____ are white, and he's wearing a grey ⁴_____ .

6 **Write a short text about what you are wearing today.**

_____

_____

_____

7 ★★☆ **Match the questions with the answers.**

0 What do you usually wear to school?   `e`

1 Do you like buying clothes?   ☐

2 What's your teacher wearing today?   ☐

3 Does your sister like wearing shorts?   ☐

4 What do you usually wear when you're not at school?   ☐

5 What do you usually wear when it's cold?   ☐

a Not really. I hate shopping.

b She's wearing trousers and a jacket.

c When I'm at home, my old jumper. I love it.

d A warm coat and a hat.

e I can't choose. We all wear uniforms.

f No. She wears jeans all the time.

8 ★★★ **Choose three of the questions in Exercise 7 and write answers that are true for you.**

1 _____

2 _____

3 _____

REFERENCE

It **looks** cool.

It **sounds** great.

It **smells** awful.

It **tastes** good.

It **feels** comfortable.

SHOPS

bookshop	department store
chemist's	mobile phone shop
clothes shop	sports shop
coffee shop	supermarket

boots

shirt

jacket

jumper

trousers

Clothes

trainers

shoes

shorts

belt

dress

VOCABULARY *EXTRA*

1 Write the words under the pictures.

cap | gloves | hat | ring | ~~scarf~~ | sunglasses

0 _____scarf_____

1 _____

2 _____

3 _____

4 _____

5 _____

2 Circle the odd word out. Explain your answers.

0 gloves   ring   (sunglasses)
sunglasses – you don't wear them on your hands.

1 hat   cap   jeans
_____

2 scarf   gloves   shorts
_____

3 shirt   trousers   jumper
_____

4 sunglasses   boots   trainers
_____

OLD THINGS, NEW IDEAS!

We've all got a lot of old stuff: clothes and shoes we don't wear, toys and games we don't play with and books we don't read. We all want to buy new things, too. So what do we do with our old things? We want to hear from you. Do you throw your old things in the bin or do you recycle them? Let us know!

Kari, Sweden
Hi! I give my old things to second-hand shops, where people can buy them and reuse them. Today, I'm at the world's first recycling shopping mall in Sweden! There are clothes, books and sports shops, but they ONLY sell second-hand things. The shops look nice and modern, and they're always busy. Right now, I'm taking a box of old things to one of the shops in the mall and then I want to buy some things for my room – all second-hand, of course!

🗨 5   ♡ 20   ⇄ 9

Jay, New Zealand
Hello there! It's my school holidays now and I'm helping at a repair centre for technology that people don't use anymore. People bring their old phones and computers to the centre. We clean and fix them and then we give them to schools, libraries and hospitals. I enjoy working on these machines, and I'm helping other people, too. It's a great way to give old stuff a new life.

🗨 8   ♡ 11   ⇄ 15

Rosalie, Canada
Do you know about Freecycle? When you have something you don't want anymore, for example, a skateboard, you post a photo of it on the Freecycle website. People go on the website and look at the things. If they want your skateboard, they contact you and you give it to them. It sounds easy and it is! My family uses Freecycle a lot. My brother and I are helping our mum add some photos of our old toys to the website at the moment. That way other children can have fun with them. Freecycle helps people save money and it helps the planet because your old things don't go into the rubbish bin!

🗨 4   ♡ 9   ⇄ 8

1 _____

2 _____

3 _____

📖 READING

1 **Read the text and write the name of the teenager under each photo.**

2 **Read the text again and answer the questions.**

1 Where does Kari take her old things?
_____

2 What does Kari plan to buy at the shopping mall?
_____

3 What is Jay doing in his school holidays?
_____

4 Why does Jay like being at the centre?
_____

5 What kind of things do people post on the Freecycle website?
_____

6 What are Rosalie and her brother doing now?
_____

3 **CRITICAL THINKING Tick (✓) what the people in the text do with old things. Then tick the things that you and your family do.**

		Text	You
1	Exchange them for other things		
2	Give them to another person		
3	Give them to a charity		
4	Keep them		
5	Sell them online		
6	Take them to a second-hand shop		
7	Put them in a recycling bin		
8	Throw them in the rubbish bin		

4 **What do you think? What are the best ways of recycling or re-using old things?**
_____
_____

DEVELOPING Writing

An email to say what you're doing

1 **INPUT** **Read the emails and answer the questions.**

1 Where is Jon?

_____

2 Where is Evie?

_____

Luca
luca@thinkmail.com

Hi Luca,

Are you all right? I hope you're having more fun than I am right now.

Well, things are not so bad. Of course, it's a bit boring here in hospital, but the doctors and nurses are really nice, and there are three other boys in my room. I like them, and we have lots of things to talk about.

This is just a quick message because I'm typing with one hand and it isn't easy! Anyway, please answer soon. How are you? What's going on at school? How's the team doing? The doctors say no sports for me for another six weeks! That's not good.

Please say hi to everyone.

See you soon,

Jon

— ✎ ✕

Evie
evie@thinkmail.com

Hi Evie,

How are things with you? Hope everything's going well.

I'm with Leah and Zoe, and we're studying for the Maths test. Maths really isn't my favourite subject, but Leah and Zoe are giving me lots of help. We're not studying at the moment. Leah and Zoe are playing table tennis and I'm writing to you!

Are you having a good time in London? You're probably walking around a street market or window shopping. Perhaps you're buying a nice present for me! I'm just kidding!

By the way, I'm in a play at school. The first show is next Friday. I hope you can come.

Mum and Dad send their love. Write soon.

Love,

Charlotte

2 **Mark the sentences T (true) or F (false).**

0 Jon is having fun. [F]

1 Jon is visiting friends in hospital. [ ]

2 The four boys in the hospital don't know what to talk about. [ ]

3 Jon isn't happy that he can't play in the team for a long time. [ ]

4 Leah, Zoe and Charlotte are taking a break from studying. [ ]

5 Charlotte is in London now. [ ]

6 Charlotte likes acting. [ ]

3 **ANALYSE** **Read the emails again. <u>Underline</u> the verbs in the present continuous and (circle) the verbs in the present simple.**

4 **PLAN** **You are going to write an email to a friend who is away from school this week. Complete the plan with your ideas.**

Ask how your friend is.

_____

Tell him/her what you are doing at the moment.

_____

Tell him/her what is happening at school this week.

_____

Ask your friend a few questions about what he/she is doing.

_____

Ask him/her to write soon.

_____

Finish with an appropriate ending.

_____

✎ WRITING TIP: informal emails

- Use informal, friendly language in emails and messages to friends and family.
- Begin by asking how the other person is. (*How are you?, How are things with you?, Are you all right?, I hope everything's (going) well.*)
- You can use informal expressions. (*I'm just kidding, How cool is that?, What a shame!*)
- To change the subject, use phrases such as *By the way, Anyway*.
- Say what you would like the other person to do. (*Write soon., Let me know …, Say hi to …*)
- End your email with an informal phrase. (*Love / Lots of love, Talk/Speak/ See you soon, or simply Bye.*)

5 **PRODUCE** **Write your email to your friend using your notes in Exercise 4 and the information in the Writing tip. Write 100–120 words.**

🎧 LISTENING

1 🔊 **2.03** **Listen to the conversations and complete the sentences.**

1 The girl wants to buy a pair of ⁰ *jeans* .
She wants them in ¹_____ .
She wants to ²_____ them on.

2 The boy is interested in a ³_____ .
It's £ ⁴_____ . He thinks it's ⁵_____ .

3 The man is looking for ⁶_____ . The shop assistant thinks he wants a book from the ⁷_____ section.
The section that the man needs is ⁸_____ him.

2 🔊 **2.03** **Complete the conversations. Then listen again and check.**

Conversation 1

> Have you got these jeans in black?
> Can I try them on, please? | Usually an 8.

Man	Hello. Can I help?
Girl	Yes. ¹_____ ?
Man	Let me look … What size are you?
Girl	²_____ .
Man	Just a moment. Here you are.
Girl	Thank you. ³_____
Man	Of course. The changing rooms are over there, on your right.

Conversation 2

> OK, thanks. | This T-shirt, how much is it?
> That's too much.

Woman	Hi. Can I help you?
Boy	Yes. ¹_____
Woman	Let me check. Here you go … it's £24.50.
Boy	Ah, OK. ²_____
Woman	Well, have a look at the T-shirts over there. They're not as expensive!
Boy	³_____

Conversation 3

> Oh, sorry. I think you need | Is there anything I can do
> Right behind you. | Yes, of course.

Woman	¹_____ for you?
Man	Hello. Have you got any books on photos?
Woman	²_____ They're in the art section over there. There are loads of books with beautiful photos.
Man	I didn't mean a book of photos. I want to learn to take good photos.
Woman	³_____ the hobbies section.
Man	Right. Where's that?
Woman	⁴_____

Train to TH!NK

Exploring numbers

3 **Read the text. Can you work out how Logan finds the answer to the teacher's questions so fast? Check with the answer at the bottom of the page.**

> **Note:**
> Even numbers:
> 2 4 6 8 …
> Odd numbers:
> 1 3 5 7 …

Logan is brilliant at Maths. One day, his Maths teacher asks the class how quickly they can find the sum of the first 50 odd numbers. The other kids are starting to think when Logan calls out, '2,500!' The teacher thinks that Logan was just lucky. 'OK,' she says, 'let's make it a bit more difficult. Who's fastest at finding the sum of the first 75 odd numbers?' Everybody is thinking hard. But 15 seconds later, Logan calls out, '5,625!' He's right again. The teacher is puzzled. How does Logan do it?

4 **A question for you: what's the sum of the first 66 odd numbers?**

_____

> **Answer**
> It's easy to calculate the sum of a series of consecutive odd numbers that start with 1. Look!
> • What's the sum of the first three odd numbers? Easy! Just multiply 3 × 3. The answer: 9!
> • What's the sum of the first nine odd numbers? Again, not difficult. Just multiply 9 × 9!
> • So to get the sum of the first 50 odd numbers you have to multiply 50 × 50, etc.

A2 Key for Schools

🎧 LISTENING
Part 1: 3-option multiple choice

1 🔊 2.04 **For each question, choose the correct answer.**

1 What number is Harry's house?

A ☐   B ☐   C ☐

2 What time does Tim's school start?

A ☐   B ☐   C ☐

3 What is in Rachel's bag?

A ☐   B ☐   C ☐

---

2 🔊 2.05 **For each question, choose the correct answer.**

1 What's the weather like?

A ☐   B ☐   C ☐

2 Which is Anne's dog?

A ☐   B ☐   C ☐

3 Where is Marco from?

Brazil   Chile   Portugal

A ☐   B ☐   C ☐

4 How far is Jasmine's house from her school?

3 km   5 km   7 km

A ☐   B ☐   C ☐

5 What is Luke's favourite sport?

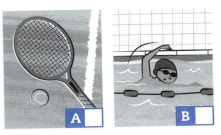 

A ☐   B ☐   C ☐

EXAM GUIDE: LISTENING PART 1

In A2 Key for Schools Listening Part 1, you hear five short conversations and then have to choose the correct picture to answer a question.

- Before you listen, look at the pictures and think about the words you will probably hear. These are the words you need to listen for.
- When there are numbers or times in the pictures, practise saying them to yourself in your head before you listen.
- Don't choose the first picture you hear. Often, you will hear the words in all three pictures. You need to listen carefully to choose the right one.
- Don't worry if you don't get the answer the first time you listen. You will hear each conversation twice.
- If you get the answer on the first listening, use the second time to check it.

CONSOLIDATION

🎧 LISTENING

1 🔊 **2.06** Listen to Annie talking about her hobby. Which of these items is not in her collection? Tick (✓) the box.

☐ ☐

☐ ☐

2 🔊 **2.06** Listen again. Answer the questions.

0 What is Annie's hobby and how is it different from other teenagers'?
Her hobby is shopping for clothes. It's different because she collects old clothes from the 1970s.

1 Who buys the clothes that Annie wears every day?
_____

2 Where does Annie buy the things for her hobby?
_____

3 Why is her collection quite small?
_____

4 Where does she keep her collection?
_____

5 Why doesn't she wear these clothes?
_____

🔤 VOCABULARY

3 Unscramble the words in *italics*.

0 Can you go to the *rapumkerest* and get some milk?   *supermarket*

1 If you're cold, put on a *premuj*.   _____

2 Look! The screen's broken. I'm going to the *bomlie enpoh hpos*.   _____

3 Mum, I need some new *reatrins*. These have got holes in them.   _____

4 The new *prentatmed toser* is really big. You can buy everything there.   _____

5 Put some *hostrs* on. It's really hot today.   _____

6 If your hands are cold, put on your *levsog*.   _____

7 My mum's a doctor. She works at the local *sopithal*.   _____

🔍 GRAMMAR

4 Rewrite the sentences to include the words in brackets.

0 I get up late on Saturday mornings. (never)
I never get up late on Saturday mornings.

1 Dad's in the bath again. (singing)
_____

2 That sounds a great idea. (like)
_____

3 My dog runs after birds in the park. (always)
_____

4 Polly like hot food, but she's eating your curry. (doesn't)
_____

5 Mum cooks at the weekend. (usually)
_____

6 Why are you drinking the coffee? It awful. (tastes)
_____

7 I like music, but I'm enjoying listening to this! (not)
_____

8 I go swimming on Sunday mornings. (sometimes)
_____

9 My mum likes most fruit, she doesn't like apples. (but)
_____

10 James loves this band, but he isn't the concert. (enjoying)
_____

5 Complete the text with the present simple or present continuous of the verbs.

Hi Archie,

I'm in Madrid and I ⁰ **'m having** (have) a great holiday. It's a wonderful place. At the moment I ¹_____ (sit) in a café with Jennie and I ²_____ (write) you a postcard. We ³_____ (eat) a paella and it ⁴_____ (taste) amazing. We ⁵_____ (watch) some dancers in a square. The women ⁶_____ (wear) really beautiful flamenco dresses. The music ⁷_____ (sound) great and the dancers ⁸_____ (look) so cool. Talking of cool – all the teenagers ⁹_____ (ride) electric scooters. But they ¹⁰_____ (not make) much noise, so you have to be careful. Anyway, bye for now. The waiter ¹¹_____ (walk) over to our table with our ice cream!

DIALOGUE

6 🔊 2.07 Complete the conversation with the words in the list. Then listen and check.

| careful | cool | do | looks | making |
| much | ~~on~~ | problem | right | up |

Ben Come ⁰ _**on**_ , Sara. Stop looking at the shoes.

Sara But they're really ¹_____ .

Ben But we're here to buy George a present. Remember?

Sara Because it's his birthday tomorrow.

Ben That's ²_____ . Now, he really likes ³_____ models, so …

Sara What about this ship?

Ben Interesting. How ⁴_____ is it?

Sara £200.

Ben What? We've only got £10.

Sara Oh. So let's forget the ship, then.

Ben Hey, that aeroplane ⁵_____ good.

Sara What are you ⁶_____ to, Ben?

Ben I'm just getting this aeroplane off the shelf.

Sara Ben – don't ⁷_____ that.

Ben It's OK. Don't worry.

Sara Be ⁸_____ .

(CRASH!)

Oh, too late. I think we've got a ⁹_____ !

📖 READING

7 Read the text about Joanna. Mark the sentences T (true) or F (false).

I've got an unusual hobby and I think it's really cool. What is it? Circus skills! Yes, that's right. I'm learning the tricks they do in circuses – like acrobatics, juggling with balls and other things! People often think I want to work in a circus – I don't! I just love doing the tricks.

Why do I like it? Because it's fun and I move a lot. I spend all day sitting down at school, so I like being active in my free time. You need to be very fit to do circus skills. Also, I'm learning new things all the time, and I feel really good when I can do a new trick.

I go to Circus School twice a week after school. Each lesson is two hours. At the moment, we're learning to ride a unicycle (that's a bike with only one wheel). It looks easy, but it's really difficult, believe me!

I practise my skills all the time at home – sometimes my parents ask me to stop! My friends want me to teach them the tricks, but they're my secret!

0 Joanna has got a typical hobby. [F]

1 She wants to be in the circus. ☐

2 She rarely learns new tricks. ☐

3 She goes to Circus School more than once a week. ☐

4 Riding a unicycle isn't difficult. ☐

5 She often does circus tricks for her family. ☐

6 She's teaching her friends new tricks. ☐

✏️ WRITING

8 Write a short text about your hobby (120–150 words). Include this information.

- What it is.
- When and where you do it.
- Why you like doing it.

3 WE ARE WHAT WE EAT

Grammar rap!

▶08

GRAMMAR
Countable and uncountable nouns → SB p.32

1 ⭐☆☆ (Circle) the correct words.

0 The books *is* / *are* on my desk.

1 The milk *is* / *are* in the kitchen.

2 There *is* / *are* three English lessons this week.

3 The cheese *is* / *are* old.

4 These apples *is* / *are* very good!

5 The music *is* / *are* loud.

6 My homework tonight *is* / *are* easy.

7 There *is* / *are* water on the floor.

2a ⭐☆☆ Write the words in the correct columns.

apple | book | cheese | homework
lesson | milk | money | water

Countable	Uncountable
apple	*cheese*
_____	_____
_____	_____
_____	_____
_____	_____
_____	_____
_____	_____

2b ⭐☆☆ Now write these words in the correct columns.

butter | computer | juice | pencil | potato | shirt

a / an / some / any → SB p.32

3 ⭐☆☆ Complete the sentences with *a* / *an* or *some*.

0 I'd like _some_ strawberries, please.

1 We've got _____ lesson at 10 o'clock.

2 There are _____ pears in the kitchen.

3 This is _____ old recipe book.

4 Let's make _____ orange juice.

5 I'd like _____ cheese sandwich, please.

6 Can I have _____ tea, please?

7 You've got _____ nice shirts!

4 ⭐⭐☆ Complete the conversation with *some* or *any*.

Dad It's Mum's birthday tomorrow. Let's make a cake for her.

Alex Yeah, great idea. What do we need?

Dad Well, first we need ⁰ _some_ sugar and ¹_____ butter.

Alex What about fruit?

Dad We're going to make a banana cake, so we need ²_____ bananas.

Alex OK. But we've got ³_____ oranges and strawberries here as well. Can we use them, too?

Dad Well, maybe we can put ⁴_____ strawberries on the top of the cake, but I'm sure we don't need ⁵_____ oranges. It's a banana cake, Alex!

Alex OK. Oh, it's going to be a great cake, Dad. But don't forget the candles. A birthday cake isn't right if there aren't ⁶_____ candles on it.

Dad That's true!

Alex So, can we please put ⁷_____ candles on it?

Dad Sure. Now – what do we do first?

Alex I can look online to get ⁸_____ information about making cakes. OK?

Dad No, we haven't got time for that. Come on – let's start.

(how) much / (how) many / a lot of / lots of → SB p.32

5 ⭐⭐⭐ Complete the sentences with *much* or *many*.

0 How _many_ desks are there in your classroom?

1 My school hasn't got _____ classrooms.

2 How _____ butter do we need?

3 Lola hasn't got _____ friends.

4 I haven't got _____ time before dinner.

5 How _____ legs has a spider got?

6 How _____ ice cream is there in the fridge?

7 We haven't got _____ homework tonight.

6 ★★☆ **Replace *a lot of* with *much* or *many*.**

0 There isn't a lot of sugar in my coffee. <u>much</u>

1 There aren't a lot of people here. _____

2 I haven't got a lot of friends. _____

3 You haven't got a lot of music on
your phone. _____

4 Please don't buy a lot of crisps. _____

5 I haven't got a lot of money in my wallet. _____

6 Hundreds of people went to the concert,
but there weren't a lot of teenagers. _____

7 There isn't a lot of information in this book. _____

too many / too much / not enough + noun

→ SB p.35

7 ★☆☆ **Complete the sentences with the words in the list.**

> a lot of clothes | a lot of people | a lot of traffic
> too many clothes | too many people | ~~too much traffic~~

0 I can't cross the road – there's <u>*too much traffic*</u> !

1 I've got _____ . I think I'll give some old
ones away.

2 I bought _____ yesterday.

3 We'll get there easily – there isn't _____
today!

4 I can't get on the bus – there are _____
on it!

5 I was really happy because _____
came to see my play.

8 ★★☆ **the correct options.**

0 I can't go out tonight – *I haven't got enough /
I've got too much* homework to do.

1 Let's do it later. *There isn't enough / There's too much*
time now.

2 We need to go shopping; *there isn't enough /
there's too much* food for tonight.

3 We can't sit down because *there aren't enough /
there are too many* chairs.

4 I need to tidy my room – *there aren't enough /
there are too many* things on the floor!

too + adjective, (*not* +) adjective + *enough*

→ SB p.35

9 ★★☆ **Complete the sentences with the phrases in the list.**

> not old enough | ~~not tired enough~~
> not warm enough | too tired | too warm

0 I can't go to sleep – I'm ____ <u>*not tired enough*</u> ____ .

1 Sorry, you're only 12. You're
_____ to see this film.

2 I'm _____ to go out tonight!
I just want to go to bed!

3 What? Go for a swim in the sea? No way!
The water's _____ .

4 I don't want to go running today. It's very sunny,
so it's _____ to run.

GET IT RIGHT!

a lot of / lots of

We use *of* + noun after *a lot* and *lots*.

✓ There are **a lot of / lots of** restaurants in my town.

✗ There are ~~a lot~~ restaurants in my town.

✓ We've got **a lot of / lots of** water.

✗ We've got ~~lots~~ water.

We use *a* before *lot of* but not before *lots of*.

✓ There are **a lot of / lots of** tomatoes in the fridge.

✗ There are ~~a lots of~~ tomatoes in the fridge.

Correct the sentences.

0 There is lots food to eat.
<u>*There is lots of food to eat.*</u>

1 We have a lot of sandwiches and a lots of fruit.
_____

2 We don't have much of milk.
_____

3 There aren't a lot places to park the car.
_____

4 Jo buys lots cakes and a lot ice cream.
_____

🔤 VOCABULARY
Food and drink

→ SB p.32

1 ★☆☆ **Complete the puzzle. What is the 'mystery word'?**

0	c	h	i	c	k	e	n
1							
2							

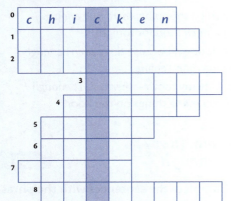

The mystery word is _____ .

Adjectives to talk about food

→ SB p.35

2 ★★★ (Circle) **the word that does not follow the adjective.**

0	roast	a chicken	b potatoes	c strawberries
1	grilled	a soup	b fish	c meat
2	boiled	a carrots	b potatoes	c salad
3	fried	a pasta	b chicken	c onions
4	salty	a soup	b tuna	c cake
5	hot	a water	b fruit juice	c chocolate

3 ★☆☆ **Complete the adjectives. Then check in the word list on page 31.**

0 de_l_icious
1 di__gu__ __in__
2 fa__ __y
3 fr__ __h
4 ho__ __ib__ __ __

5 s__ __t__
6 s__ __ cy
7 s__ee__
8 ta__ __y

4 ★★☆ **Look at the words in Exercise 3. Match them with the definitions.**

0 it has a very nice taste (2 words)
 ____*delicious, tasty*____
1 it has a very bad taste (2 words)
 _____
2 it has a lot of fat in it _____
3 it has sugar in it _____
4 it has a hot and strong taste (for example, curry)
 _____
5 it is in a natural condition (not from a tin or frozen)
 _____
6 it has a lot of salt in it _____

5 ★★☆ **Invent two dishes, one that you think is really delicious, and one that you think is really disgusting.**

Delicious – a burger with mushrooms and cheese
Disgusting – chocolate ice cream with tuna and onions

WordWise: *have got*

→ SB p.33

6 ★☆☆ **Match the sentences with the pictures.**

a I've got a problem.
b I've got a headache.
c I haven't got time.
d I've got something to do.

7 ★★☆ **Match these sentences with a–d in Exercise 6.**

0 'Do you have another bag?' — a
1 'I need to rest.'
2 'I want to do it now.'
3 'I have a piano lesson in 10 minutes.'

REFERENCE

FOOD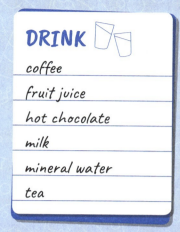

bread	fish	sausages
burgers	green beans	soup
carrots	ice cream	steak
cake	mushrooms	strawberries
cereal	onions	tacos
cheese	pancakes	tomatoes
chicken	pasta	tuna
chocolate	peppers	yoghurt
eggs	salad	

DRINK

coffee

fruit juice

hot chocolate

milk

mineral water

tea

WORDS THAT GO TOGETHER

roast vegetables	fried chicken	cheese and mushroom omelette	chocolate cake
boiled potatoes	grilled fish	tomato soup	tuna sandwich

DESCRIBING FOOD

delicious	fresh	savoury	tasty
disgusting	horrible	spicy	yummy
fatty	salty	sweet	

EXPRESSIONS WITH *HAVE GOT*

have got a headache	have got something to do	have got my reasons
have got time	have got a problem	

VOCABULARY *EXTRA*

1   Complete the words with the missing letters.

0 b *i s c* u i *t*

1 __ u t __ e r

2 h __ __ __ __ y

3 __ i __

4 r i __ __

5 s __ __ d w __ __ h

2   Complete the sentences with your ideas. Use the names of food or drinks.

1 I really like _____ ,
_____ and _____ .

2 I don't like _____ ,
_____ or _____ .

3 I eat _____ , _____
and _____ every day.

4 I think _____ , _____
and _____ are healthy.

What food do people eat on national days and festivals in your country? Let us know in the comments below.

CELEBRATING WITH FOOD!

CHILE EN NOGADA

Hi, I'm Alejandra and I'm from Mexico.

On 16 September, we celebrate Independence Day with a special dish called *chile en nogada*. We eat it on this day because this dish has the same colours as the Mexican flag: green, white and red! The main ingredient is a large green chilli pepper with meat, vegetables, fruit and spices inside it. There's a white sauce over the pepper and some red fruit seeds on top. Everyone loves this dish, so we make enough for all the family and that takes a long time!

MOONCAKES

Hello! I'm Li-Na from China.

We have a festival for the first full moon of autumn and some people call it the Mooncake Festival! Mooncakes are round like the moon and they look beautiful. Inside there is a sweet cream which is often made from red beans. Yes, beans in a dessert! And it tastes really good. Families get together on this special day. At night, we go outside to look at the moon, eat mooncakes and drink tea – lots of tea. How many cakes do we eat? Too many – because they are so delicious!

HAGGIS

Hi there! I'm Duncan from Scotland.

We always eat haggis on 25 January, Burns' Night, to celebrate the birthday of a Scottish poet, Robert Burns. Haggis is simple food made with cheap ingredients: sheep meat, vegetables and cereals – boiled in a sheep's stomach! I know, it sounds disgusting – but it's really tasty!

On Burns' Night, the haggis is at the centre of the celebrations. We stand and listen to Scottish music when my mum puts it on the table. My dad reads a famous Robert Burns' poem about a haggis, then we sit down and enjoy a good dinner.

READING

1 Read the article and match photos 1–3 with photos a–c.

2 Read the article again and mark the sentences C (chile en nogada), M (mooncakes) or H (haggis).

0 It's part of a Chinese tradition. **M**

1 You eat this dish to celebrate a writer. ☐

2 There are a lot of ingredients in this. ☐

3 These have sugar in them. ☐

4 The colour of the food is important. ☐

5 You drink something hot with this food. ☐

6 This food doesn't cost much to make. ☐

3 CRITICAL THINKING Think about your country. Complete the table with examples of traditional food and drinks that people have on special days.

Celebration	
Savoury food	
Sweet food	
Drinks	

4 Is food a big part of your country's traditions? Number these things in order (1 = very important, 6 = not very important) for your country.

Clothes	
Food	
Sport	
Stories/poems	
Music	
Festivals	

DEVELOPING ⟩ *Writing*

A recipe

1 **INPUT** **Read the recipe for mushroom and red pepper omelette.**

1 How long does it take to make?

_____

2 How many people is it for?

_____

MUSHROOM AND RED PEPPER OMELETTE

🕐 **Time: 20 minutes**   👤 **Serves 1**

What you need (ingredients)

2–3 eggs	Oil
100 g mushrooms	Milk
Half a small onion	Salt
Half a red pepper	Pepper

How to make it (method)

1 Wash and **slice** the mushrooms, onion and red pepper.

2 **Heat** a tablespoon of oil in a frying pan and **add** the vegetables. **Stir** and cook for about 10 minutes.

3 **Beat** the eggs with some milk, salt and pepper.

4 When the vegetables are ready, put them on a plate.

5 Heat another tablespoon of oil in the frying pan. When it's hot, add the eggs.

6 Put the vegetables on half of the omelette. Then cover them with the other half of the omelette.

Serve with a salad.

2 **Read the recipe again. Answer the questions.**

0 What do you cook first?
the vegetables

1 How long do you cook the vegetables?

_____

2 What do you add to the eggs?

_____

3 When do you cook the egg mixture?

_____

3 **Read the section 'How to make it' again. Match the verbs in bold with these definitions.**

0 put an ingredient with the other ingredients _*add*_

1 move round with a spoon _____

2 make something hot _____

3 cut into thin pieces _____

4 mix quickly with a spoon or fork _____

4 **ANALYSE** **Tick (✓) the correct answer.**

All the verbs are in:

☐ the present simple

☐ the imperative

☐ the present continuous

✏️ WRITING TIP: a recipe

- Choose a simple dish you know how to make (*a sandwich, a cake*).
- Write a list of the ingredients.
- Think of the actions you need to take to make your dish and write down the verbs (*wash, slice*).
- Use the verbs to write short, simple instructions.
- Look up the new words you need in a dictionary.

5 **PLAN** **Write a plan for your recipe. Organise the information in three sections.**

Name, number of servings and cooking time	
Ingredients	
Instructions	

6 **PRODUCE** **Write the recipe using your plan in Exercise 5.**

🎧 LISTENING

1 🔊 **3.01** **Listen to the conversation between Sally and Maggie. Tick (✓) the things that Sally puts in her dish.**

beans	☐	carrots	☐
chicken	☐	chilli peppers	☐
garlic	☐	meat	☐
mushrooms	☐	onions	☐
potatoes	☐	red peppers	☐
tomatoes	☐		

2 🔊 **3.01** **Listen again. Mark the sentences T (true) or F (false).**

0 Sally is cooking something for dinner. ☐ T

1 Sally thinks her recipe is new. ☐

2 The onions, tomatoes and red peppers are grilled together. ☐

3 Sally's dish isn't spicy. ☐

4 Sally uses fried meat. ☐

5 They can eat Sally's food with salad and potatoes. ☐

6 Maggie thinks *chilli con carne* is from Mexico. ☐

7 *Chilli con carne* usually has mushrooms in it. ☐

DIALOGUE

3 **Put the words in order to make phrases.**

0 OK / It's _____ *It's OK.* _____

1 sorry / I'm / really _____

2 really / I / bad / feel _____

3 it / worry / Don't / about _____

4 **Use the phrases in Exercise 3 to complete the conversation. There may be more than one possible answer.**

A Ella, do you remember that I borrowed your book?

B Yes, I remember. Why?

A Well – I can't find it. I haven't got it any more.
   ⁰_____ *I'm really sorry* _____ .

B Oh, ¹_____ , Jared. It's not a very good book!

A ²_____ , Ella. I want to buy another one for you.

B No, Jared. ³_____ . Really. Look – I've got an idea.

A What?

B There's a film of the book now. It's at the cinema this weekend. Come with me to see it!

A Oh, OK then. Thanks.

PHRASES FOR FLUENCY   → SB p.36

5 🔊 **3.02** **Put the sentences in order to make a conversation. Then listen and check.**

A ☐ Well, they're from France. They're going to be here for a couple of weeks.

B ☐ Oh really? What is it?

A ☐ Some friends are coming next week to visit me.

B ☐ So what?

A ☐ 1 Hey, Fiona. I've got some news.

B ☐ Great. I love parties!

A ☐ Oh, I'm sorry, Fiona, I didn't mean to. Of course, I want you to come as well.

B ☐ What about me? Don't forget me!

B ☐ OK. Some French people are here in our town! That's good news.

A ☐ Yes, it is. I want to have a party when they're here.

A ☐ Me too! I'm going to invite Joe, and Charlie, and Lily, and Holly, and … .

6 🔊 **3.03** **Complete the conversations with the words in the list. Then listen and check.**

> ~~Actually~~ | a couple of | as well
> So what | upset with | What about me

1 **A** Do you like this curry?
   B Yes, it's delicious. ⁰_____ *Actually* _____ , curry's my favourite food, I think. But I like other things ¹_____ , of course.

2 **A** I'm going to the cinema with ²_____ friends.
   B ³_____ ? Can I come, too?

3 **A** John's very angry with you.
   B ⁴_____ ? I don't like him anyway.

4 **A** Katy isn't talking to me.
   B Perhaps she's ⁵_____ you.
   A Probably, but I don't know why.

> **PRONUNCIATION**
> Vowel sounds: /ɪ/ and /iː/ Go to page 118. 🎧

📖 READING AND WRITING
Part 2: 3-option multiple matching

1 For each question, choose the correct answer.

	Jenna	Ethan	Alice
1 Who can't eat one type of food?	A	B	C
2 Who wants a job making food?	A	B	C
3 Who likes doing exercise?	A	B	C
4 Who is often very hungry?	A	B	C
5 Who prepares food for other people?	A	B	C
6 Who enjoys going out to eat?	A	B	C
7 Who doesn't eat much sweet food?	A	B	C

TALKING ABOUT FOOD

Jenna
I eat a lot because I need enough energy to swim! I swim three times a week and enter lots of competitions. I eat a healthy diet with a lot of fruit, vegetables, fish and pasta. But I don't eat many cakes and biscuits. After swimming practice, I'm always really hungry, so I eat bananas and drink a lot of water.

Ethan
I love cooking. I want to be a top chef when I grow up! I help with the cooking at home. I really enjoy making dinner with my mum or dad, because we chat while we're cooking. I usually make lunch for my sisters too when my parents are out at work. This year, I'm doing a cooking course after school, so I'm learning a lot of new recipes.

Alice
I'm careful about the food I eat because I can't eat food with milk in it. There's milk in a lot of food you buy, so I always read the ingredients! I know what I can and can't eat. My parents buy special milk made from nuts and I put it on cereals and in hot drinks. I love going to vegan restaurants because I know I can eat everything there.

EXAM GUIDE: READING AND WRITING PART 2

In A2 Key for Schools Reading and Writing Part 2, there are three short texts on the same topic and seven questions. Each question is about one of the texts and you have to choose the correct text, A, B or C.

- Read the title. This can help you understand the texts.
- Then read the three texts quickly for general comprehension.
- Read the first question and look for this information in the three texts.
- Circle the letter that corresponds to the text.
- You don't usually find the same words in the question and the texts, so look for words and phrases with similar meanings.
- Sometimes the questions summarise part of the text.

4 ALL IN THE FAMILY

Grammar rap!

▶11

Ⓖ GRAMMAR
Possessive adjectives and pronouns

→ SB p.40

1 ★☆☆ Circle the correct words.

⁰I / **My** name's Raul. ¹I / My family is quite big. There are ²I / my three sisters, Vicky, Mila and Madison, and ³we / our have got two brothers, Dylan and Edward, so there are three boys and three girls. ⁴Us / Our sisters love playing football for the school team. ⁵They / Their team is really good. Vicky is ⁶they / their goalkeeper. ⁷She / Her friends think she's the best goalkeeper in the world. ⁸Us / Our mum and dad love football too, so on Sundays we all go and watch the three girls play. Dad's got a brother. ⁹He / His name's Jonathan. He sometimes goes with us to watch the girls play. Uncle Jonathan often says to me, ¹⁰'You / Your sisters are good footballers, but I'm sure you are better.' I think that's funny.

2 ★★☆ Rewrite the sentences using possessive pronouns.

0 Is this your dog? ___*Is this dog yours?*___

1 Is that his car? _____

2 Are these your jeans? _____

3 Is this my sandwich? _____

4 Are these our seats? _____

5 Is that her house? _____

whose and possessive *'s*

→ SB p.40

3 ★☆☆ Rewrite the sentences. Use the word(s) in brackets and put the apostrophe in the correct position.

0 A Whose is this skateboard?
B It's his. (Peter) ___*It's Peter's.*___

1 A Whose are those books?
B They're theirs. (my friends) _____

2 A Is this your umbrella?
B No, it's hers. (Mrs Miller) _____

3 A Are those your brothers' bikes?
B No, they're theirs. (my sisters) _____

4 A Is this John's phone?
B No, it's his. (Tom) _____

5 A Whose are these keys?
B They're hers. (Sandra) _____

4 ★★☆ Circle the correct words.

0 A Can you check **who's** / whose at the door?
B It's **Matt's** / Matt friend, Henry.

1 A Who's / Whose house is this?
B It's the Taylor's / Taylors' new house.

2 A Is it Sam / Sam's bike?
B No, it's his sister Polly / Polly's.

3 A Our teacher's / teachers son is a doctor.
B You mean Mrs Smith's / Smith son?

4 A Who's / Whose your favourite band?
B I really like Imagine Dragons' / Dragon's songs a lot.

5 A Who's / Whose are these comics?
B They aren't mine. I think they're James / James's.

5 ★★★ Complete the conversations.

1 A I really like ⁰___*your*___ jacket, Rob.
It looks really good on ¹_____ .
B ²_____ isn't ³_____ .
It's Theo's. He lent it to ⁴_____ .
I've got to give it back to ⁵_____ later.

2 A Do you know the Richard twins?
⁶_____ live next to Sally. In fact she lives at number 9, and ⁷_____ house is number 11.
B Yes, I know Sally. My sister is a good friend of ⁸_____ . She's a friend of mine, too.

3 A I'm sure that's Liam's dog over there. So where is ⁹_____ ? He never goes anywhere without ¹⁰_____ dog.
B It's not ¹¹_____ . Liam's dog is black and that one is brown.

4 A Hey, what are ¹²_____ doing, Henry? That's ¹³_____ sandwich. It's not ¹⁴_____ !
B I'm sorry. ¹⁵_____ was hungry. Here ¹⁶_____ are. Don't be angry with ¹⁷_____ , OK?

5 A ¹⁸_____ is this camera?
B Let's ask Jim. I think it's ¹⁹_____ . Or talk to Ruby. Maybe it's ²⁰_____ .

PRONUNCIATION
-er /ə/ at the end of words   Go to page 119.

was / were

→ SB p.43

6 ★☆☆ (Circle) the correct words.

0 Breakfast this morning (was) / were delicious, but the bananas wasn't / (weren't) very sweet.

1 Mrs Donald, our English teacher, was / were really cool yesterday. We was / were happy, too.

2 My parents wasn't / weren't at home yesterday evening. They was / were at my school with my teacher.

3 I was / were really hungry but there wasn't / weren't any sandwiches left.

4 The film was / were really boring. We wasn't / weren't very interested in it.

5 They was / were very late. There wasn't / weren't many people left at the party.

7 ★☆☆ Complete the sentences with was or were.

0 A __Was__ it cold this morning?
   B Cold? Not really.

1 A _____ Victor and Daniel born in the same year?
   B No. Victor is 9, Daniel is 11.

2 A _____ your cousin angry with you?
   B Not at all.

3 A _____ all your friends at your party?
   B Only Tyler wasn't. He was ill.

4 A _____ Caitlin hungry?
   B Yes, very, very hungry.

5 A _____ they at home?
   B No, they're still at school.

8 ★★☆ Complete the conversation between the police officer (PO) and Eddie. Use was, wasn't, were or weren't.

PO So, just let me check your story again.

Eddie Sure.

PO Your mum and dad [0] __were__ outside.

Eddie Yes, they [1] _____ . They [2] _____ in the garden.

PO And your brother [3] _____ in the garden, too.

Eddie No, he [4] _____ . He [5] _____ in the garage. He [6] _____ very happy because his bike [7] _____ broken.

PO And [8] _____ your sister, Jess, in the house?

Eddie Yes, she [9] _____ . She [10] _____ in the kitchen. She [11] _____ very hungry.

PO And the twins? [12] _____ they in the kitchen with her?

Eddie No, they [13] _____ . They [14] _____ in the living room, in front of the TV.

PO And you, Eddie. Where [15] _____ you?

Eddie I [16] _____ tired, and I [17] _____ very well. I [18] _____ in bed.

PO Sleeping.

Eddie Yes, I [19] _____ asleep.

PO So, if you [20] _____ asleep, how do you know where everyone was?

9 ★★☆ Answer the questions so they are true for you.

1 Were you at school yesterday at 3 pm?
_____

2 Was it hot yesterday?
_____

3 Was your teacher angry this morning?
_____

4 Were you in bed early last night?
_____

5 Were you late for school last week?
_____

6 Was your best friend happy to see you this morning?
_____

GET IT RIGHT!

it's and its

We use **it's** as a short form of **it is**. We always use an apostrophe (') between **it** and the **-s**.

✓ It's my mum's birthday today.

✗ Its my mum's birthday today.

We use **its** to talk about possession when the subject is an object or an animal*. **Its** never has an apostrophe.

✓ This book is very old. **Its** pages are yellow.

✗ This book is very old. It's pages are yellow.

*We sometimes use his/her to talk about animals that are our pets.

Put four apostrophes (') in the correct place.

I love my new phone. I love the colour. Its red. Its my favourite colour. The screen is big, and the camera takes good pictures. My sister loves her phone because of its modern design and its apps, and because its small. Her friends gave it to her for her birthday. Its really nice, but I think mine is better.

VOCABULARY
Family members → SB p.40

1 ★★☆ Complete the puzzle. What is the 'mystery word'?

⁰U	N	C	L	E

(crossword grid with numbered rows 1–6)

0 My mum's brother is my …
1 My brother is my parents' …
2 My sister is my parents' …
3 My parent's daughter is my …
4 Mum is my dad's …
5 My dad's sister is my …
6 Grandpa is my grandma's …

The mystery word is _____ .

2 ★★★ Use each word to write a sentence that is true for your family.

0 sister-in-law
My aunt Caroline is my dad's sister-in-law.

1 big sister
_____
_____

2 daughter
_____
_____

3 cousins
_____
_____

4 grandpa
_____
_____

5 uncle
_____
_____

6 little brother
_____
_____

7 aunt
_____
_____

Feelings → SB p.43

3 ★★☆ Unscramble the words in the list. Write them under the pictures.

> deliever | drewori | droup | credas
> cusdefno | estup | g̶r̶a̶n̶y̶ | purerissd

0 _____*angry*_____

4 _____

1 _____

5 _____

2 _____

6 _____

3 _____

7 _____

4 ★★☆ How do you feel when …

0 you watch a horror film?
I feel scared!

1 you get low marks in a test?
_____

2 you get top marks in a test?
_____

3 you don't understand a lesson?
_____

4 your best friend forgets your birthday?
_____

5 you've got an important test in the morning?
_____

6 a test is over (and it wasn't so difficult)?
_____

7 your grandparents give you some money (and it's not your birthday)?

REFERENCE
Family members

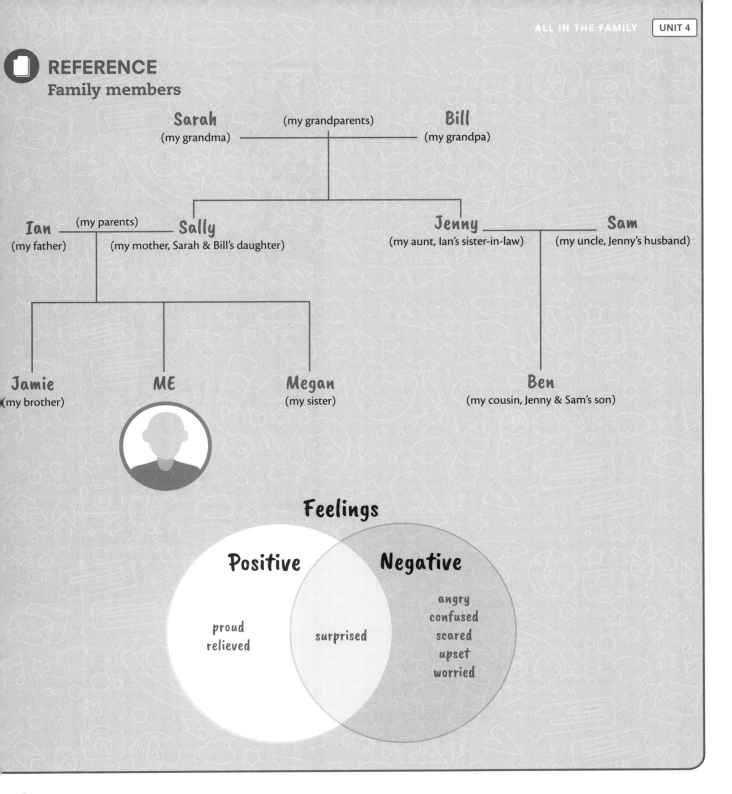

Sarah (my grandma) ——— (my grandparents) ——— Bill (my grandpa)

Ian (my father) ——— (my parents) ——— Sally (my mother, Sarah & Bill's daughter)

Jenny (my aunt, Ian's sister-in-law) ——— Sam (my uncle, Jenny's husband)

Jamie (my brother)

ME

Megan (my sister)

Ben (my cousin, Jenny & Sam's son)

Feelings

Positive

proud
relieved

surprised

Negative

angry
confused
scared
upset
worried

VOCABULARY *EXTRA*

1 Complete the word families with words from the list.

~~grandchild~~ | granddaughter | grandson | nephew | niece | stepbrother

Grandparents' family	Uncle and aunt's family	Step-family
⁰ *grandchild* (m/f)	³ _____ (m)	stepmother
¹ _____ (m)	⁴ _____ (f)	stepfather
² _____ (f)		stepsister
		⁵ _____ (m)

2 Draw your family tree. Write the names of all the people and their relationships to you.

📖 READING

1 Read the TV guide quickly and complete the sentences.

1 Joe is Lucy's _____ . **2** John is Paul's _____ .

2 Read the TV guide again. For each question, choose the correct answers for sentences 1–7.

0 *We're Watching You* is on twice a week.
  A Right **B** Wrong **C** Doesn't say

1 There are famous actors in the show.
  A Right **B** Wrong **C** Doesn't say

2 The show makes the reviewer laugh.
  A Right **B** Wrong **C** Doesn't say

3 The families behave badly for the camera.
  A Right **B** Wrong **C** Doesn't say

4 No one in the Collins family is happy with what they watch.
  A Right **B** Wrong **C** Doesn't say

5 Anna Collins is good at sport.
  A Right **B** Wrong **C** Doesn't say

6 The Lawson family like action films.
  A Right **B** Wrong **C** Doesn't say

7 Saturday nights don't usually have a happy ending for the Lawsons.
  A Right **B** Wrong **C** Doesn't say

3 Answer the questions.

0 Why do people like watching the show?
  Because it's really funny.

1 What does Joe and Lucy's dad like watching?
  _____

2 What does Joe's sister want?
  _____

3 Whose grandpa can't hear very well?
  _____

4 What does John's grandson want to do?
  _____

4 **CRITICAL THINKING** Match the members of the Collins family with the sentences.

1 'I'm going to my room to read.' ☐
2 'Can we watch the tennis match?' ☐
3 'This is boring! Let's watch *The Simpsons*!' ☐
4 'Where's the remote control?' ☐

a Dad **b** Mum **c** Lucy **d** Joe

5 What happens in your family when you watch television? Are they similar to anyone in the Collins family?

My sister only watches cartoons. She's similar to Joe.
_____
_____

TV GUIDE:
WE'RE WATCHING YOU

Watching TV families watching TV

We're Watching You is a simple but brilliant idea: put a tiny camera on the front of the TV in several family homes and record them, and then make it into a TV programme. And that's all it is, a TV programme that shows us real people watching real TV. Exciting? Not really. But it is really, really funny.

Of course, all the people on the show know that a camera is recording them, but they soon forget it's there, and then the fun starts.

There are the Collins family from Huddersfield. Mike, the dad, can never find the remote control, and soon starts shouting at his kids, Joe and Lucy, to find it. Of course, as his wife, Anna, says, he always finds it – he is usually sitting on it! Anna only wants to watch sport, but her husband wants cooking programmes, Joe wants cartoons and Lucy wants a quiet house without TV. No one usually gets what they want.

And then there's the Lawson family from Taunton. They sit down together and watch a film every Saturday night. It always starts off well, but soon there are problems. Grandpa John can't hear very well. He always wants to turn the volume up. This upsets his daughter, Georgia, who hates the loud noise. So Grandpa turns it down, but then he asks his grandson, Paul, to tell him what people are saying. This makes Paul angry. And then his mum often walks in front of the TV into the kitchen to get a cup of tea. Poor Paul – he doesn't want a cup of tea, he just wants to watch the film.

We're Watching You is fun to watch, but I'm glad these cameras aren't in my home!

DEVELOPING Writing

An invitation

1 **INPUT** **Read the invitations. Put the events in the order that they start on Friday.**

 The visit to a friend's home   ☐ The film   ☐ The concert   ☐ The party

A

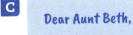

Hayden
Hayden@thinkmail.com

Hayden,

Can you come to my party at The Fun Factory? It's on Friday evening from 8 pm to 11 pm. They do food, so don't eat before you get there! Please let me know if you can come because The Fun Factory need to know the number of people. Hope you're free on Friday.

Best,

Noah

C

Dear Aunt Beth,

There's a concert at my school next Friday and I'm in it. Would you like to come? It starts at 6.30 pm, but get there early if you want a good seat. My school is at the beginning of Brook Lane. There's a lot of space to park. Hope to see you there.

Daisy

B

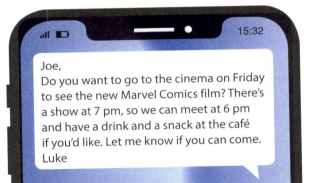

15:32

Joe,
Do you want to go to the cinema on Friday to see the new Marvel Comics film? There's a show at 7 pm, so we can meet at 6 pm and have a drink and a snack at the café if you'd like. Let me know if you can come.
Luke

D

Jasmine
Jasmine@thinkmail.com

Hi Jasmine,

I'm so happy it's the holidays! How about coming to my house this Friday? We can come and pick you up at about 10 am and take you back in the evening. Please say 'yes'. I've got lots of video games. We'll have fun.
Bella
PS My mum says you have to ask your parents first.

2 **ANALYSE** **Look at the lines from the replies. Match them with the invitations.**

0 Mum and Dad want me back before dinner if that's OK.   ☐ D

1 By the way, what sort of food do they do?   ☐

2 I can be there at 6 pm. I want a seat right in the front row!   ☐

3 Sorry, I'd love to see it, but I can't be there at that time. Could we go on Saturday instead?   ☐

✏ WRITING TIP: an invitation

- Invitations don't need to be long, but they need to contain all the important information – day, time and place.
- In invitations to friends, we use friendly, informal language. Use expressions to make the person feel very welcome. (*Please come, I hope you can come, Please say 'yes'.*)
- In formal invitations, begin with *Dear ...* and use expressions like *Would you like to ... ?* instead of *Do you want to ...?*
- Don't forget to ask the person to reply.

3 **PLAN** **Choose TWO situations and plan your invitations.**

1 You want your uncle to come and watch your band play on Friday evening.

2 You want your best friend to go to the adventure park with you on Saturday.

3 You want your friend to go away with you and your family for the weekend.

Invitation 1
What? _____
When? _____
Where? _____
Other information _____

Invitation 2
What? _____
When? _____
Where? _____
Other information _____

4 **PRODUCE** **Write your invitations using your notes in Exercise 3. Write 50–60 words for each invitation.**

 LISTENING

1 🔊 **4.02** Listen to the conversations. In each conversation, someone is asking for permission to do something. Tick (✓) the conversation if they get permission to do it.

Conversation 1 ☐
Conversation 2 ☐
Conversation 3 ☐

2 🔊 **4.02** Listen again. Choose the correct answer A, B or C.

Conversation 1

0 Aaron wants to go to his friend's house by

A car.　　**B** bike.　　**C** bus.

1 Holly is … of her bike.

A scared　　**B** tired　　**C** proud

Conversation 2

2 Joshua is

A doing his homework.

B going out.

C playing video games.

3 His mum is … about his school work.

A angry

B surprised

C worried

Conversation 3

4 Who does the girl want to invite to her house?

A her grandparents

B some school friends

C her cousins

5 What does the girl decide to change?

A the day

B the place

C the time

3 **Put the words in order to make questions and answers.**

1 A I / your / Can / borrow / bike?

Can I borrow your bike?

B it / very / OK, / but / with / be /careful

_____

2 A out / I / please? / now, / go / Can

_____

B come / can / but / home / You / go, / early

_____

3 A some / friends / Can / Saturday? / I / round / on / invite

_____

B can't / No, / sorry, / I'm / you

_____

DIALOGUE

4 Write a conversation for each of these pictures Use a request in each conversation, with a positive answer in one, and a negative answer in the other.

Tom _____

Finley _____

Tom _____

Finley _____

Poppy _____

Mum _____

Poppy _____

Mum _____

Train to TH!NK

Making inferences

5 Look at the text on page 40 again. Who do you think says these things? Choose from the names in the list.

Anna | Georgia | Joe | John | Lucy | Mike | Paul

0 What did he say?　　　　　　　*John*

1 It's my turn and I want to watch football. ____

2 Can't we just turn it off? ____

3 Shh! They're giving us a really good recipe for a cake. ____

4 You're probably sitting on it, as usual. ____

5 No, Mum, I don't want anything to eat, thank you! ____

6 Where is it? I want to change channel. ____

7 Can you turn it up a bit? ____

8 Not tennis again. I want to watch *Batman*. ____

9 Please – turn it down! ____

A2 Key for Schools

📖 READING AND WRITING
Part 5: Open cloze

1 For each question, write the correct answer. Write ONE word for each gap.

> **Lizzy**
> lizzy@thinkmail.com
>
> Hi Lizzy,
> How ⁰ _are_ you?
> I'm really happy because some family from Australia are staying ¹_____ us at the moment. I ²_____ only seven the last time they were here! My cousins are called Ethan ³_____ Grace. We are having ⁴_____ great time together – except they're on holiday, and I'm at school! In Australia, it's their summer holiday now.
> I'd like to invite some of my friends ⁵_____ meet them at my house on Saturday afternoon.
> Can ⁶_____ come then? I hope so!
> Let me know.
> Love
> Daisy

EXAM GUIDE: READING AND WRITING PART 5

In A2 Key for Schools Reading and Writing Part 5, you have to complete six gaps in a short email or message with ONE word. There is always one example for this task.

- Read the text quickly and focus on general understanding. Don't worry about the gaps at this stage.
- First, look at the example carefully.
- Now start with the first gap. Remember to read the complete sentence and especially the words before and after the gap.
- Think about one word that you could write in the gap and try it.
- If you can't think of a word, try thinking about the type of word you need: verb, adverb, subject, preposition, article, question word and so on.
- When you have completed all the gaps, re-read the text and make sure it makes sense.

🎧 LISTENING
Part 3: 3-option multiple choice

1 🔊 4.03 For each question, choose the correct answer. You will hear Olivia talking to her friend Dave about her family.

1 Where is Beth's husband from?
 A France   **B** Scotland   **C** Ireland
2 Olivia has got
 A one sister   **B** two sisters   **C** three sisters
3 How old is Luke?
 A 8 weeks old   **B** 8 months old   **C** 8 years old
4 What is Olivia's grandpa called?
 A Roger   **B** Tony   **C** William
5 Dave thinks Olivia looks like her
 A cousin   **B** mother   **C** father

EXAM GUIDE: LISTENING PART 3

In A2 Key for Schools Listening Part 3, you will hear a longer dialogue. You have to choose the correct option, A, B or C, for each of the five questions.

- Before you listen, read through all the questions. This will tell you what the listening is about.
- Look at each question carefully and identify the kind of information you need to listen out for.
- The questions are in the same order as the dialogue, so they are easy to follow.
- You'll hear the conversation twice. Use the second time to listen for missing answers and check the answers you already have.

2 🔊 4.04 For each question choose the correct answer. You will hear Liam talking to his friend Rachel about a new restaurant.

1 The new restaurant is
 A French.   **B** Italian.   **C** Mexican.
2 The restaurant is in
 A High Street.   **B** River Street.   **C** Bridge Street.
3 When did Rachel go to the restaurant?
 A on Thursday
 B on Wednesday
 C at the weekend
4 How much was Rachel's meal?
 A £9   **B** £9.50   **C** £10
5 Rachel was there
 A with her family.
 B in the afternoon.
 C for her birthday.

CONSOLIDATION

🎧 LISTENING

1 🔊 4.05 **Listen to the conversation. Choose the correct answer A, B or C.**

  1 What does the man want to drink?
    A pineapple juice
    B water with ice and lemon
    C water without ice and lemon

  2 What does the woman want to drink?
    A mineral water
    B tea
    C lemonade

  3 Which sandwich does the man want?
    A tuna
    B chicken
    C cheese and tomato

2 🔊 4.05 **Listen again and answer the questions.**

  0 Why does the man order mineral water?
    Because there isn't any apple juice.

  1 What does the waitress bring the man?
    _____

  2 Whose is the drink?
    _____

  3 Why can't the man get the sandwich he wants?
    _____
    _____

  4 What does he think about the café?
    _____
    _____

  5 Where does he arrange to meet Lisa?
    _____
    _____

Ⓖ GRAMMAR

3 Ⓒircle **the correct word.**

  0 **A** Is that your cousins' house?
    B Yes, it's *ours* / *theirs.*

  1 **A** Is that your tablet?
    B No, it's *her* / *hers.*

  2 **A** Is that your grandpa's watch?
    B Yes, it's *his* / *hers.*

  3 **A** Has your school got *it's* / *its* own swimming pool?
    B No, we go to the sports centre.

  4 **A** Do you like your new phone?
    B Yes, I do and *it's* / *its* easy to use, too.

  5 **A** *Whose* / *Who's* are those trainers?
    B They're mine.

4 Ⓒircle **the correct words.**

Natalie	⁰*Was* / Ⓦere you at the cinema with Jenni and Edie last night?
Joseph	Yes, I ¹*was* / *were*. It ²*was* / *were* a lot of fun.
Natalie	And then ³*was* / *were* you all at the café opposite the cinema later?
Joseph	How do you know? We ⁴*was* / *were*, actually.
Natalie	We were there too, so I also know what you had. You always have ⁵*some* / *any* fish and ⁶*a lot of* / *much* chips, and you don't eat ⁷*some* / *any* green vegetables.
Joseph	Yeah, I know. I don't eat ⁸*too much* / *enough* healthy food, you're right.
Natalie	Hey, I've got an idea. Come and have lunch at our place. My dad's a good cook. He's a vegetarian, so he doesn't cook ⁹*some* / *any* meat, but he makes ¹⁰*much* / *lots of* excellent salads.
Joseph	Thanks, that sounds good.
Natalie	Well, come tomorrow at 12.30.
Joseph	Great, thanks.

🔠 VOCABULARY

5 **Unscramble the adjectives in brackets. Complete the sentences.**

  0 How would you like your vegetables, *boiled* (deilob) or *grilled* (llrigde)?

  1 This curry is too _____ (ypisc) for me, I'm afraid.

  2 I'm sorry, but this smells so _____ (unstsdgiig) that I can't eat it.

  3 **A** Do you think the soup's too _____ (aslyt)?
    B No, not at all. I think it's very _____ (yttas).

  4 This steak is nice, and the salad's _____ (cidesliou).

  5 **A** How do you like the _____ (staro) chicken?
    B It's absolutely _____ (uymym).

  6 These vegetables are all really _____ (hefrs).

  7 This cheesecake isn't very nice. It's too _____ (weset), and it tastes a bit _____ (igorbn).

6 Complete the sentences. Write the words for family members and complete the words for feelings.

0 I've got a present for my _little sister_ (I'm her big brother). She'll be very __surprised__ when she sees it!

1 My _____ (mother's father) loves taking photos. He's really p_____ of a photo of my sister playing.

2 My _____ (uncle's wife) was in hospital for a few days. We're all r_____ that she's OK again.

3 My _____ (uncle's daughter) Joanna hates horror films. They make her really s_____ .

4 Roy and his _____ , Christina, (he's her husband) are u_____ because their daughter Caroline never visits them.

DIALOGUE

7 🔊 **4.06** **Complete the conversation. Use the phrases in the list.**

> a couple of | ~~can I borrow~~ | can I, please
> don't worry | feel really bad | I'm so sorry
> of course | that's OK | upset with | what about

Zoe Jordan, ⁰_____ _can I borrow_ _____ your umbrella?

Jordan ¹_____ you can. Your big brother never says 'no', does he?

Zoe That's right. Thanks so much. Bye.

Jordan Where are you going?

Zoe I'm going to meet Mia and Emily.

Jordan And ²_____ my umbrella? Are you taking it with you?

Zoe ³_____ ? It's raining. It's only ⁴_____ hours. I'll be back soon.

Jordan ⁵_____ . But make sure you bring it back. I'll be very ⁶_____ you if you don't!

Later …

Jordan Ah, you're back.

Zoe Well, yes, but I ⁷_____ . I left your umbrella on the bus.

Jordan I can't believe it.

Zoe ⁸_____ , Jordan. It was an accident.

Jordan OK, ⁹_____ . These things happen. But next time … I'll say 'no'!

📖 READING

8 Read the magazine article about unusual birthday traditions. Mark the sentences T (true) or F (false).

HAPPY BIRTHDAY AROUND THE WORLD

How do you celebrate your birthday? With a cake, a party for your friends, with games and fun for all? In some countries birthday celebrations are really unusual.

In some parts of India, for example, on a child's first birthday, the parents cut off the child's hair. This happens to both boys and girls, and there is a party to celebrate.

In Vietnam, they celebrate everybody's birthday on New Year's Eve. Parents give their children a paper envelope with coins in it – 'lucky money'.

In Korea, they celebrate day number 100 after the child is born. Children get rice cakes with honey and red and black beans. Families make sure a child gets a lot of these rice cakes. When a child gets a 100 rice cakes, this means that they will live a long, happy life.

When children in Denmark wake up on their birthday, there are presents all around the bed. Some children are so excited that they find it difficult to fall asleep the night before!

0 Parents in some parts of India cut off their children's hair on their first birthday ☐ T

1 Only Indian boys have a haircut on their first birthday. ☐

2 In Vietnam they celebrate children's birthdays on the last day of the year. ☐

3 In Korea they celebrate before a child is four months old. ☐

4 Children in Korea get lots of rice cakes with chocolate and ice cream. ☐

5 In Denmark children get their presents the night before their birthday. ☐

✏️ WRITING

9 Write a paragraph about how you celebrate your birthday (about 80–100 words). Use these questions to help you.

- How important are birthdays in your family?
- How do you celebrate them?
- Are there any interesting traditions?

5 NO PLACE LIKE HOME

Grammar rap!

▶14

GRAMMAR

Past simple (regular verbs) → SB p.50

1 ★☆☆ **Find nine more verbs in the puzzle and write them next to the past forms.**

S	T	A	Y	D	U	T	S	T	W	L
T	W	T	R	E	V	I	R	R	A	P
O	R	M	D	V	E	S	U	T	N	A
P	L	A	N	K	L	I	K	E	T	S
L	I	R	E	R	R	V	A	R	N	W

0 _____stay_____ stayed
1 _____ liked
2 _____ arrived
3 _____ planned
4 _____ dried
5 _____ studied
6 _____ wanted
7 _____ visited
8 _____ stopped
9 _____ used

2 ★★☆ **Complete the sentences with the past simple verbs in Exercise 1.**

0 The bus _arrived_ 30 minutes late.

1 We _____ to go to the beach.

2 The test was really important, so I _____ all weekend for it.

3 I really _____ the film. It was so funny.

4 We _____ my uncle in Spain when we were on holiday.

5 We _____ in a really expensive hotel on our last holidays. It was great.

6 She _____ playing football because of an accident.

7 I _____ my birthday party very carefully. I wanted it to be perfect.

8 My hair was wet, so I _____ it with your towel.

3 ★★☆ **Write the past simple of the verbs.**

0 call _____called_____
1 start _____
2 try _____
3 seem _____
4 watch_____
5 enjoy _____
6 love _____
7 ask _____
8 finish _____
9 look _____
10 show _____
11 decide _____

4 ★★★ **Complete the story with the past simple of the verbs in brackets.**

When I was younger I [0] _loved_ (love) LEGO. My sister and I [1]_____ (play) with it all the time. I always [2]_____ (ask) for LEGO for my birthday. I was a member of the LEGO Club. Every three months a magazine [3]_____ (arrive) in the post. It was full of ideas for models you could build, and there were photos of models from club members. Each time I [4]_____ (open) the magazine, I [5]_____ (look) at that page for hours. I [6]_____ (dream) of seeing one of my models on that page. One day, my sister and I [7]_____ (decide) to build the best model ever and send a photo to the magazine. For days we [8]_____ (work) on it. We [9]_____ (use) so many different types of bricks, big ones, small ones, square ones, round ones, red ones, blue ones – every shape and colour you can imagine. After about a week we [10]_____ (finish). It was amazing and we were so happy. Then we [11]_____ (need) to take a photo of it. Very carefully I [12]_____ (pick) it up and [13]_____ (carry) it down the stairs. My sister [14]_____ (open) the kitchen door and there were three more steps to the kitchen table. Unfortunately, the dog was sitting between me and the table. He [15]_____ (jump) up and [16]_____ (knock) the model to the floor. It [17]_____ (smash) into thousands of pieces. We [18]_____ (try) to fix it but it was useless. I [19]_____ (look) at my sister and we both [20]_____ (realise) it was the end of our dream

PRONUNCIATION
Regular past tense endings Go to page 119.

Modifiers: *quite, very, really*   → SB p.51

5 ★★☆ **Rewrite the sentences to include the words in brackets.**

0 I'm not happy today. (very)
I'm not very happy today.

1 Your grandmother is young. (really)
_____

2 Hurry up. We're late. (very)
_____

3 Can I have a sandwich? I'm hungry. (quite)
_____

4 I'm tired. I want to go to bed. (quite)
_____

6 ★★☆ Circle the correct word.

0 It's 40°C today. It's *quite /* really hot!

1 That song's OK. It's *quite / very* good.

2 This bed is so uncomfortable. It's *quite / very* hard.

3 The sea's *quite / very* cold today. Don't go swimming – you'll freeze!

4 That food is *quite / really* delicious. I want to eat it all.

Past simple negative   → SB p.53

7 ★☆☆ **Match the beginnings of the sentences to the end parts of the sentences.**

0 I chatted with her for an hour,   `c`

1 He downloaded the game,   ☐

2 She posted the card on Monday,   ☐

3 He cooked them a really special meal,   ☐

4 The team played really well,   ☐

a but it didn't arrive for my birthday.

b but we didn't win.

c but we didn't talk about you.

d but they didn't really like it.

e but it didn't work.

8 ★★☆ **Make the sentences negative.**

0 I liked the ice cream.
I didn't like the ice cream.

1 We enjoyed the film.
_____

2 They went to France for their holidays.
_____

3 She wanted to go to the party.
_____

4 He won 1st prize in the photography competition.
_____

5 You met Danielle at my party.
_____

9 ★★★ **Complete Jenny's holiday blog with the past simple of the verbs in the list.**

arrive | ask | not know | not work
not understand | order | promise | stop

🏠 HOME   ❓ ABOUT   📰 NEWS   ✉ CONTACT

DAY 8 PIZZA IN ROME

We ⁰_____*arrived*_____ in Rome last night at about 7 pm. Dad really wanted to see the Trevi Fountain straight away. I did too, but I was really hungry after the long journey. Dad ¹_____ we could get pizza after we saw the fountain, so we decided to go. The fountain was OK but it was far too busy. I ²_____ it was so popular. Then Dad ³_____ an Italian couple to take a picture of us, using his terrible Italian. That was quite embarrassing! They ⁴_____ him at all! Luckily my brother speaks Italian, so he translated for Dad and we got a great photo. On our way back to the hotel, we finally ⁵_____ at a pizza restaurant for dinner. I ⁶_____ a mushroom pizza and it was delicious. The best pizza ever. Anyway, we arrived back at the hotel at about 10 pm. I tried to connect to the WiFi, but it ⁷_____ , so I just went to bed and dreamed about pizza all night.

GET IT RIGHT!

Past simple (regular verbs)

We usually add *-ed* to verbs ending in vowel + *-y*.

✓ *play – played*

✗ *play – plaid*

If the verb ends in consonant + *-y* (e.g. *try*), we change the *-y* to *-i* and add *-ed*.

✓ *try – tried*

✗ *try – tryed*

The exceptions to this rule are *pay* and *say*:

pay – paid

say – said

Correct the past simple forms.

1 plaid   _____

2 staid   _____

3 studyed   _____

4 tryed   _____

5 enjoied   _____

6 tidyed   _____

 **VOCABULARY**
Furniture

→ SB p.50

1 ★★☆ **Complete the crossword.**

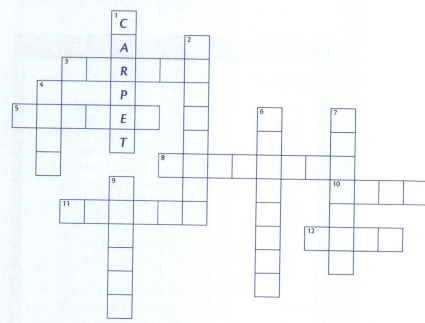

→ SB p.50

ACROSS

3 Nico is looking at his hair in the … .

5 Liam is standing in front of the … in the kitchen making dinner.

8 Alfie is putting his clothes back in the … .

10 Don't turn the … off. I'm using it to read.

11 Jessica is washing her hair in the … .

12 Ollie is doing his homework at his … .

DOWN

1 The dog is lying on the … in front of the TV.

2 Mum is sitting in an … reading the newspaper.

4 Rebecca is sitting with Susanna and Julia on the … .

6 Mum is closing the … because it's getting dark now.

7 Dad is putting all his books up on the … .

9 Can I use the … before we go out? Yes, it's in the bathroom upstairs.

2 ★★★ **What are your favourite pieces of furniture? Choose three and write about each one.**

I love the armchair in our living room because it's very comfortable.

1 _____

2 _____

3 _____

Adjectives with -ed and -ing

→ SB p.53

3 ★☆☆ **Find nine more adjectives in the word snake and write them below.**

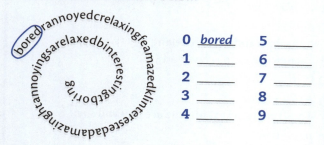

0 *bored* 5 _____

1 _____ 6 _____

2 _____ 7 _____

3 _____ 8 _____

4 _____ 9 _____

4 ★★☆ the correct words.

0 This sunset is *amazing* / *amazed*.

1 This lesson is *boring* / *bored*.

2 I love holidays. They're so *relaxed* / *relaxing*.

3 We broke Mr Evans's window with our ball. I think he is a bit *annoying* / *annoyed* with us.

4 I passed the exam! I'm *amazing* / *amazed*.

5 Don't turn the TV off, Dad. This programme is really *interesting* / *interested*.

WordWise: Phrasal verbs with *look*

→ SB p.51

5 ★☆☆ **Match the questions with the replies.**

0 What are you looking at? | d

1 What does 'circulation' mean? | ☐

2 Do you know why your laptop stopped working? | ☐

3 Do you want to come to my house after school? | ☐

4 What are you looking for? | ☐

a I don't know. Let's look it up in the dictionary.

b I can't. I've got to look after my little sister.

c My pen. I can't find it anywhere.

d Some old photos.

e No – it's a mystery. I'm still looking into it.

6 ★★☆ Circle **the correct words to complete the sentences.**

0 The police are looking *into* / *after* / *up* / *for* what happened last night.

1 I looked *after* / *up* / *for* / *at* the address of the museum on the internet.

2 Look *up* / *for* / *at* / *into* that bird. It's amazing.

3 My mum and dad are looking *for* / *to* / *into* / *after* a new house.

4 She helps her dad look *at* / *into* / *after* / *up* her little brothers.

REFERENCE

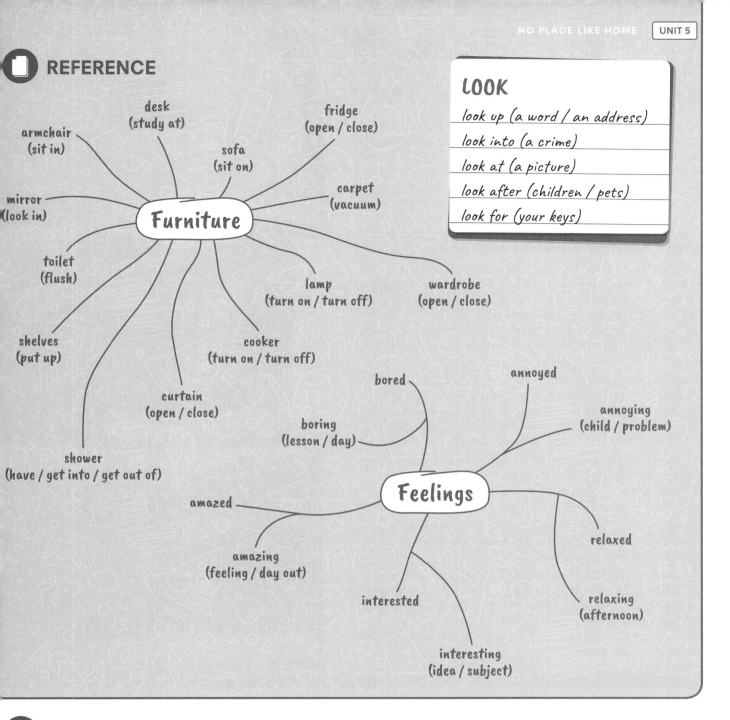

LOOK

look up (a word / an address)

look into (a crime)

look at (a picture)

look after (children / pets)

look for (your keys)

Furniture

desk (study at)
fridge (open / close)
armchair (sit in)
sofa (sit on)
carpet (vacuum)
mirror (look in)
toilet (flush)
lamp (turn on / turn off)
wardrobe (open / close)
shelves (put up)
cooker (turn on / turn off)
curtain (open / close)
shower (have / get into / get out of)

Feelings

bored
annoyed
boring (lesson / day)
annoying (child / problem)
amazed
relaxed
amazing (feeling / day out)
interested
relaxing (afternoon)
interesting (idea / subject)

VOCABULARY *EXTRA*

1 Complete Toby's list of chores with the words in the list.

~~bookcase~~ | clock | cupboard | microwave | sink | washing machine

0 Put the dictionary back in the ___bookcase___ .

1 Wash the dirty dishes in the _____ .

2 Put the dirty clothes in the _____ .

3 Take the hot food out of the _____ .

4 Put the clean dishes back in the _____ .

5 Put a new battery in the _____ .

2 Write the names of all the furniture and appliances in these rooms in your home.

Kitchen _____

Bathroom _____

Living room _____

Bedrooms _____

Your bedroom _____

BIG HOUSES,
SMALL HOUSES

1 _____

Some of us live in big houses, some of us live in small houses. Some of us live in apartments in very tall buildings, some of us live in bungalows next to the sea. But most of us live in houses that look like … well … houses. But not everyone. Some people like things that are a bit different, and that includes their homes. For example, there's a house that looks like a strawberry in Japan, another one that looks like a mushroom in Ohio, US, and there's a toilet-shaped house in South Korea. There's even a house in Poland that is completely upside down!

Maybe you know the children's poem about the old lady who lived in a shoe. In Pennsylvania, US, there is a real shoe house. Of course, it's not really a shoe, just a house in the shape of a shoe. A local shoe manufacturer called Mahlon N. Haines had the idea of building it. He used it as a guesthouse. When he died it became an ice cream shop for a while. These days, it's a museum.

2 _____

The One Log House in Garberville, California, US, is a one-bedroom house inside the trunk of a 2,000-year-old giant redwood tree. It took two people seven months to remove all the inside of the tree and make a living space that is just over two metres high and nearly 10 metres long.

Joanne Ussary from Benoit, Mississippi, in the US, lives in a plane. It's a Boeing 727 without the wings. The plane cost $2,000 and it cost another $4,000 to move it on to her land. She spent another $24,000 making it into a home.

It's not the only 'flying' home in the US. In Chattanooga, Tennessee, there is a house in the shape of a spaceship: a round white disc with four legs.

And believe it or not, there is a walking house in Denmark. It's a hexagonal tube supported by six metal legs. It can move over most surfaces. It is a collaboration between Danish artists and scientists. Moving home couldn't be any easier. When you want to live somewhere new, just push a button and walk your house to a new location.

3 _____

 **READING**

1 Read the article quickly. Then write the names of the countries under the photos.

2 Read the article again. Answer the questions.

   0 What is the shoe house in Pennsylvania today?
     It's a museum.

   1 How old is the tree trunk of the One Log House?
     _____

   2 How much did Joanne Ussary spend on turning the plane into a home?
     _____

   3 Who built the walking house in Denmark?
     _____

   4 Which two houses have legs and how many legs have they got?
     _____

   5 How many houses in the article are in the US?
     _____

3 CRITICAL THINKING **Choose an alternative title for this article.**

  a My dream home
  b Coming home
  c Homes with a difference
  d Celebrity homes

4 What's important to you in a home? Number these things in order (1 = very important, 6 = not very important).

  ☐ A garden
  ☐ Big rooms
  ☐ Comfortable furniture
  ☐ Modern electrical gadgets
  ☐ Nice colours
  ☐ Your own room

DEVELOPING Writing

A blog post

1 **INPUT** **Read the blog post. Tick (✓) the things that Mark writes about.**

☐   ☐   ☐   ☐   ☐

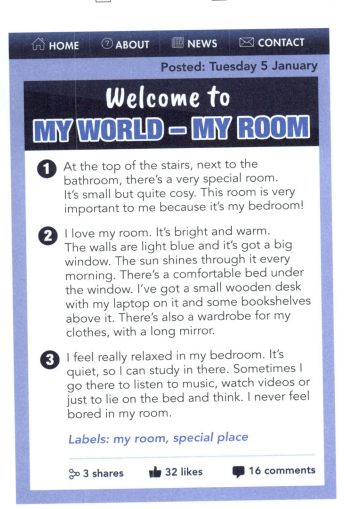

⌂ HOME   ② ABOUT   📰 NEWS   ✉ CONTACT

Posted: Tuesday 5 January

Welcome to MY WORLD – MY ROOM

① At the top of the stairs, next to the bathroom, there's a very special room. It's small but quite cosy. This room is very important to me because it's my bedroom!

② I love my room. It's bright and warm. The walls are light blue and it's got a big window. The sun shines through it every morning. There's a comfortable bed under the window. I've got a small wooden desk with my laptop on it and some bookshelves above it. There's also a wardrobe for my clothes, with a long mirror.

③ I feel really relaxed in my bedroom. It's quiet, so I can study in there. Sometimes I go there to listen to music, watch videos or just to lie on the bed and think. I never feel bored in my room.

Labels: my room, special place

⤻ 3 shares   👍 32 likes   💬 16 comments

2 **Circle the correct words.**

0 Mark's room is *big* / *small.*
1 The walls are *blue* / *white.*
2 His bed is *large* / *comfortable.*
3 He's got a *wooden* / *glass* desk.
4 His room is *quiet* / *noisy.*

✏ **WRITING TIP: adjectives**

- Use adjectives to describe things. Adjectives give more information about things and make our writing more interesting.
- Adjectives go <u>before</u> nouns. (*a long mirror*)
- If there is more than one adjective before the noun, they usually go in this order: opinion, size, colour, material. (*a lovely big room; a red plastic chair; a comfortable blue bed*)

3 **ANALYSE** **Look at the three paragraphs of Mark's blog. Which paragraph …**

a describes the room?   ☐
b talks about how the room makes Mark feel?   ☐
c introduces the room and says where it is?   ☐

4 **PLAN** **Think about your favourite room.**

1 Where is it?
_____

2 Describe it. What's in it?
_____

3 How do you feel when you are there? Why?
_____

4 Think of some good adjectives to use.
_____

5 **PRODUCE** **Write a blog post about your favourite room in about 100–130 words. Use your notes from Exercise 4 to help you.**

🎧 LISTENING

1 🔊 5.03 Tick (✓) the activity they *don't* talk about.

GIANT RAFFLE Great Prizes! **1** ☐

4 ☐

2 ☐

TALENT CONTEST **5** ☐

3 ☐

6 ☐

2 🔊 5.03 **Listen again and complete the sentences with no more than three words.**

0 The class decided to _raise money_ for people who haven't got a home.

1 Emily _____ there were so many homeless people in their town.

2 Dan wants to raise _____ money.

3 Dan thinks it is difficult to find good _____ for the raffle.

4 Emily wants the class to _____ to sell.

5 Emily suggests a concert because lots of their classmates _____ .

6 In the end, they decide to organise a _____ .

DIALOGUE

3 **Put the words in order to make sentences from the conversation.**

0 do / to / What / help / can / we
What can we do to help?

1 we / organise / sale / a / don't / Why / second-hand /
_____

2 not / so / I'm / sure
_____

3 about / a / What / raffle / having
_____

4 tickets / friends / We / family / buy / could / ask / our / and / to
_____

5 tomorrow / Let's / tell / everyone
_____

PHRASES FOR FLUENCY → SB p.54

4 🔊 5.04 **Put the sentences in order to make a conversation. Then listen and check.**

A ☐ Oh no! But I know what you mean – he gets angry really easily.

A ☐1 Did Chris invite you to his party?

A ☐ Well, I hope you come anyway.

A ☐ What did you say?

A ☐ Hang on. Why not? I thought you were friends.

B ☐ We were. But I said something he didn't like and now he isn't talking to me.

B ☐ No, he didn't. It's no big deal, though.

B ☐ To be honest, I don't want to.

B ☐ I just said he wasn't a very good singer. He got really angry with me.

B ☐ Anyway, it's not my problem he's angry. And I really don't care about his silly party.

5 **Complete the sentences with the words in the list.**

~~deal~~ | hang | honest | mean | problem | though

1 A Why are you so annoyed? It's really not a big _deal_ .
B Maybe it isn't. I'm still angry, _____ .

2 A I don't want to go to the match, to be _____ . I don't really like football.
B I know what you _____ . It's really boring.

3 A _____ on. We can't just leave this dog here on the street.
B Of course we can. It's not our _____ .

A2 Key for Schools

READING AND WRITING
Part 1: 3-option multiple choice

1 For each question, choose the correct answer.

1

Cora,
I'm afraid I won't be at dance practice – I've hurt my foot skateboarding! Please let our teacher know why I won't be there…
Michael

Why has Michael sent this message?

A To change some plans that he made with Cora.

B To ask Cora to tell the teacher about his accident.

C To find out if Cora is well enough to go to dance class.

2

ANYONE FOUND NOT PUTTING THEIR RUBBISH INTO BINS **WILL** GET INTO TROUBLE!

-Headteacher

What does the headteacher want students to do?

A To remember to keep the school tidy.

B To think about ways the school can stay clean.

C To understand that there is a problem at school.

3

James
james@thinkmail.com

Hi Alicia,
I'm having a hard time with the Maths homework for next class – especially page 109! Could you tell me how you did it?

A James is offering to help Alicia with her homework.

B James is asking Alicia if she has completed the homework.

C James would like Alicia to give him some advice on the homework.

4

COMPETITION

Post a photograph doing your favourite hobby
One entry per student

AMAZING PRIZES!

Students must upload a photo…

A of an activity they enjoy doing.

B that shows a location they like going to.

C about a subject they like learning about.

5

Jackson,
I'll be home later than usual, and won't be home for dinner. I've left you some things in the fridge to choose from.
Mum

A Jackson has to wait until his mum returns before having his dinner.

B Jackson must let his mum know what he wants to have for dinner.

C Jackson needs to decide what he prefers for his dinner.

6

MUSIC CLUB
The last meeting before tomorrow's concert is in the school theatre from 3–4pm.
Don't forget your instruments – they're still in the music room.

What is this notice saying?

A Members need to go to the theatre to collect their musical instruments.

B Members will be able to watch some of the school concert for an hour.

C Members are going to practise at a different location for the meeting.

EXAM GUIDE: READING AND WRITING PART 1

In A2 Key for Schools Reading and Writing Part 1, there are six short texts and you choose the option with the correct meaning. The texts are usually notices, notes, emails or text messages. There are three options and you choose one.

- Read the different texts.
- Take your time to look at the whole text. There's plenty of time.
- Read the three options carefully.
- Before you choose, compare the other options with the text again.
- Make your final choice.

6 FRIENDS FOREVER

Grammar rap!

▶17

GRAMMAR
Past simple (irregular verbs)

→ SB p.58

1 ★☆☆ Write the past simple of these verbs. Use the irregular verb list on page 128.

0 know	_knew_	**6** drink	_____
1 buy	_____	**7** have	_____
2 bring	_____	**8** say	_____
3 take	_____	**9** tell	_____
4 eat	_____	**10** get	_____
5 leave	_____	**11** cost	_____

2 ★★☆ Complete the crossword.

¹S A ²W

³
⁴H
O
⁵ ⁶ ⁷
⁸ T
E D
⁹
¹⁰ D
N

ACROSS

1 Yesterday we … a really good film.

4 His name is Lewis? Really? I … it was Lucas.

8 We met last year. We … really good friends.

9 It was my sister's birthday. I … her a CD.

10 Last night I … my homework.

DOWN

1 My dad played the guitar and I … a song.

2 I … to the cinema three times last week.

3 I liked the blue shirt and the red one. In the end I … the red one.

5 We had a party last night. We … a lot of noise!

6 We … a strange noise, but it was only the wind.

7 When he came in to the room, everyone … up.

8 The match … at three o'clock.

3 ★★★ Complete the text with the past simple of the verbs in brackets. (Careful! Some verbs are regular and some are irregular.)

⌂ HOME   ? ABOUT   📰 NEWS   ✉ CONTACT

It was hard to believe, but it was true – a concert by Imagine Dragons, in our town! When I
⁰___*saw*___ (see) the poster, I ¹_____ (phone) all my friends to tell them. At first they
²_____ (not believe) me, but then they all
³_____ (get) really excited!
We all really ⁴_____ (want) to go to the concert – it was our favourite band and we
⁵_____ (hear) that you could buy tickets online. The tickets were expensive, though.
I ⁶_____ (not have) enough money, but my dad ⁷_____ (give) me some money as an early birthday present, and we ⁸_____ (buy) four tickets near the stage.
We were all very excited. For two weeks we
⁹_____ (not talk) about anything else – just the concert. And then finally, the big day
¹⁰_____ (arrive). My friends ¹¹_____ (come) to my house, and we all ¹²_____ (get) ready. Then we ¹³_____ (take) a bus to get to the concert.
We ¹⁴_____ (have) a great time at the concert. The band ¹⁵_____ (play) really well and they ¹⁶_____ (perform) for three hours!
My friends and I ¹⁷_____ (sing) too, because we ¹⁸_____ (know) the words to every song!
Unfortunately they ¹⁹_____ (not sing) my favourite song, but you can't have everything, I guess.
After the show we all ²⁰_____ (go) to a new sushi place. We ²¹_____ (eat) some really tasty food and ²²_____ (talk) about the show.
Allie ²³_____ (say) it was the best concert ever – and we all ²⁴_____ (think) the same!

Double genitive

→ SB p.59

4 ★★☆ **Choose the correct words.**

0 Last week, I met a friend of ... .

  A you   **B** your   **C** yours

1 He gave me a jacket of ... .

  A him   **B** his   **C** he

2 Oh, yes, Spencer and Sue are very good friends of ... .

  A ours   **B** our   **C** us

3 I don't know her, but she's a cousin of ... .

  A Johns'   **B** John's   **C** John

4 I love their music. I've got eight CDs of ... .

  A them   **B** their   **C** theirs

5 I found out that our teacher is an old friend of ... .

  A my father's   **B** me father   **C** my father

Past simple questions

→ SB p.61

5 ★★☆ **Complete the questions with the past simple of the verbs. Then use the information in brackets to write the answers.**

0 _____ *Did you like* _____ the film yesterday? (you / like)

  _____ *Yes, I did.* _____ (✓)

1 _____ any clothes at the weekend? (he / buy)

  _____ (✗)

2 _____ a lot of photos last weekend? (you / take)

  _____ (✗)

3 _____ with you to the party? (your friends / go)

  _____ (✓)

4 Who _____ in town this morning? (you / see)

  _____ (Jenny)

5 Where _____ on holiday last year? (they / go)

  _____ (Corfu)

6 What _____ for dinner last night? (you / eat)

  _____ (fish and chips)

6 ★★★ **Complete the questions.**

0 I saw someone yesterday.

  Who *did you see* _____ ?

1 I bought something last week.

  What _____ ?

2 They went somewhere last weekend.

  Where _____ ?

3 I heard something.

  What _____ ?

4 You said something.

  What _____ ?

5 She told me something.

  What _____ ?

6 I met someone.

  Who _____ ?

7 I found the answer somewhere.

  Where _____ ?

8 I phoned her last night.

  Who _____ ?

GET IT RIGHT!

Past simple questions

We form past simple questions with question word + *did* + subject + base form of the verb. Remember to use *did* in the correct place.

✓ Where **did** you **meet** your friend?

✗ Where ~~you met~~ your friend?

✗ Where ~~you did meet~~ your friend?

Mark (✗) next to the incorrect sentences. Then write the correct sentences.

1 Why you didn't come to my party? ☐

  _____

2 What you did at the weekend? ☐

  _____

3 Where did they go on holiday? ☐

  _____

4 Who you went to the cinema with? ☐

  _____

5 What he saw at the cinema? ☐

  _____

VOCABULARY
Past time expressions
→ SB p.58

1 ★☆☆ Circle the correct words.

0 I saw her two weeks ago / yesterday.

1 Where were you last / yesterday afternoon?

2 Tom arrived last / yesterday week.

3 We started at this school five years ago / last.

4 I tried to phone you three hours ago / afternoon.

5 Chloe didn't feel well last / yesterday morning.

6 We went out last / yesterday night.

2 ★★☆ Complete the puzzle. What is the 'mystery word'?

	0	L	A	S	T		

0 We went to the cinema … Sunday.

1 The time now is 7.25. … minutes ago, it was 7.10.

2 Today is Monday. … was Sunday.

3 It's 25th August. Two … ago it was the 11th.

4 You were late for school this … .

5 We watched a great film last … .

6 I was born fifteen years … .

7 It's December. … months ago it was October.

8 We went out to a restaurant yesterday … .

The mystery word is _____ .

3 ★★★ Complete the sentences so that they are true for you.

0 Two years ago, *my sister got married* .

1 Last night, _____ .

2 Three weeks ago, _____ .

3 _____ an hour ago.

4 Ten years ago, _____ .

5 Last Sunday, _____ .

6 _____ yesterday morning.

7 Last year, _____ .

8 Yesterday afternoon, _____ .

Personality adjectives
→ SB p.61

4 ★★☆ Complete the adjectives and then match them with the definitions a–i.

0 f u n n y _____ [f]

1 _ _ _ _ p f _ _ _ [ ]

2 _ _ t _ _ _ l _ _ _ _ _ t [ ]

3 _ h _ _ _ _ f _ _ [ ]

4 _ _ _ _ y- _ _ _ _ n _ [ ]

5 g _ _ _ _ _ _ u _ [ ]

6 _ _ _ _ f _ d _ _ _ _ [ ]

7 _ _ a l _ _ _ s [ ]

8 b _ _ i _ _ _ [ ]

a relaxed and not easily worried

b happy and positive

c unhappy because you want something someone else has

d happy to give other people money, presents or time

e not interesting or exciting

f making you smile or laugh

g certain about your ability to do things well

h happy to help others

i able to learn and understand things easily

5 ★★☆ Look at these character adjectives. Write P (positive) or N (negative) in the boxes.

☐ cheerful		☐ confident
☐ easy-going		☐ funny
☐ horrible		☐ generous
☐ helpful		☐ jealous
☐ intelligent		☐ boring

6 ★★☆ Choose four adjectives from Exercise 5. Write sentences about yourself.

I'm usually a cheerful person.

I'm not really jealous at all.

_____

_____

_____

_____

> **PRONUNCIATION**
> Stressed syllables in words Go to page 119. 🎧

REFERENCE

last week   last night

last

last year

yesterday morning

yesterday

yesterday afternoon

five years ago

an hour ago

ago

two weeks ago

PERSONALITY ADJECTIVES

POSITIVE 🙂

cheerful
confident
easy-going
funny
generous
helpful
intelligent

NEGATIVE 🙁

boring
horrible
jealous

POSSESSIVE PRONOUNS

I	mine
you	yours
he	his
she	hers
it	its
we	ours
they	theirs

VOCABULARY *EXTRA*

1 **Complete the sentences with the adjectives in the list.**

friendly | ~~honest~~ | kind | lazy | patient | sensible

0 Molly is _____ honest _____ . She always tells the truth.

1 Eddie is _____ . He never does any work!

2 Our teacher is _____ . She repeats things and helps us. She never gets angry.

3 Louis is _____ . He always knows what to do and has good ideas.

4 Jayden and Carlos are _____ . They love meeting new people.

5 Felicity is _____ . She cares about other people and helps them.

2 **Think of a person you know for each adjective in Exercise 1 and write sentences.**

My best friend Kelly is very kind.

_____
_____
_____
_____
_____
_____
_____

This year a new documentary series appeared on British TV called *Young at Heart*.

The programme matched teenagers with senior citizens and asked them to meet twice a week for two months. They filmed what happened when the pairs spent time together. Two of these people were Amelia Ross and Mary Edwards.

Mary is a 76-year-old retired nurse who lives alone. She has some good friends, but they live in different cities and she doesn't see them often. She likes meeting new people and keeping fit, so she goes to salsa dancing classes twice a week. Amelia is a 14-year-old student. She loves music and wants to be a singer. In her free time, she likes chatting with her friends on her phone and watching videos online. She doesn't like sports.

Before Mary met Amelia, she didn't like teenagers very much. In her opinion, they spent too much time on their phones. Amelia thought that old people were boring and strict.

When they met for the documentary, Mary was surprised that Amelia didn't do any exercise, so she invited her to a salsa class. Amelia didn't really want to go, but she had a great time. Mary is really outgoing and they laughed a lot together. Later Amelia found out that Mary had a mobile phone but didn't know how to use it. It was still in the box! Amelia showed her how to send messages to her friends and to listen to music online. Mary didn't like the same songs as Amelia, but she enjoyed discovering new music styles. In one episode of the series, she asked Amelia to sing for her. Amelia was a bit shy, but she agreed. Mary loved her voice and said she should enter the school talent show. Amelia was nervous but she followed this advice. It was a good idea because she won first prize!

By the end of the series, Amelia and Mary were good friends. Amelia still goes to the salsa classes and Mary is an expert with her tablet now. They say they plan to keep in touch in the future.

📖 READING

1 Read the article and tick (✓) the best title.

☐ An unexpected friendship
☐ Friends forever
☐ Making friends is easy

2 Read the text again and complete the sentences with the correct name, *Mary* or *Amelia*.

0 _____*Mary*_____ doesn't live with her family.
1 _____ isn't very sporty.
2 _____ tried a new activity.
3 _____ learned to use something.
4 _____ followed her friend's advice.
5 _____ won a competition.

3 `CRITICAL THINKING` **Tick (✓) the best description of the story.**

☐ Young people don't spend enough time with old people.
☐ Friends can help each other learn new things.
☐ When friends have similar interests, age doesn't matter.

4 Think about your best friend. Write three reasons why you get on well.

_____
_____
_____
_____
_____

DEVELOPING { Writing

A thank you note

1 **INPUT** Read the thank you notes and match them with the replies. Write 1–3. There is one extra reply.

1

Hi Alfie,
Thank you so much for the concert ticket! That was so generous of you. I was really surprised when I opened your card and the ticket fell out. How did you know they're my favourite band? I can't wait for the concert! Are you going too?
Thanks again,
Ada

2

10.01

Dear Lola,
I want to thank you for finding my ring. I was so upset when I lost it. It was a present from my grandma, so it's really special to me. I thought it was lost forever. I hope you enjoy these chocolates – they're from your favourite shop!
Love,
Tilda

3

Hello Harry,
Here's your tennis racket. I was very careful with it. Thanks very much for lending it to me. It's a really good racket and I want to buy my own. Can you come to the sports shop with me to choose a good one?
See you soon,
Ed

WRITING TIP: thank you notes

- We use informal language in notes and messages to friends.
- Begin your message with *Hi* or *Hello*, and the name of the person. You can also use *Dear* (name), in informal and formal messages.
- Use short forms. (*I'm, We didn't, you aren't*)
- Make it personal by using sentences such as: *That was so generous/nice of you! How did you know it's my favourite …?, I hope you enjoy …*
- End your message with an informal phrase and your name. (*Love, Take care, See you soon*)

a ☐ Hi … ,
Thank you for giving it back to me so soon. No problem, I can help you pick one – just let me know when you want to go.

b ☐ Hello … ,
I'm glad you feel OK now. I know it's difficult but forget what she said to you. It wasn't true, and I'm sure she feels bad.

c ☐ Hi … ,
That's OK. It was on the floor in the bathroom. When I saw it, I recognised it and knew it was yours. Thanks for the present – delicious!

d ☐ Hey … ,
You're very welcome! When I saw your T-shirt with their name on it, I knew what to give you. I'm going, too! I can't wait!

3 **PLAN** Choose one of these situations and write down your ideas for a thank you note.

1 You received a birthday present.
2 Your friend lent you something.
3 You got a nice surprise.

Why you are writing _____

_____

Why you like the thing or are happy _____

_____

A personal comment _____

_____

2 **ANALYSE** Underline the expressions meaning 'thank you' in notes 1–3.

4 **PRODUCE** Write a thank you note. Include some of the phrases in the Writing tip. Write 50–60 words.

🎧 LISTENING

1 🔊 **6.03** Listen to part of a podcast. Charlie and Ava are talking about their friendship. Circle the correct words.

1 Charlie and Ava went to the same *primary* / *secondary* school.

2 Their favourite lesson was *PE* / *science*.

3 Charlie and Ava were *similar* / *different* when they were at school.

2 🔊 **6.03** Listen again. Choose the correct answer A, B or C.

1 When they met for the first time,
   A Ava didn't like Charlie.
   B they talked a lot.
   C Ava wasn't happy.

2 At school,
   A they didn't spend much time together.
   B they were interested in the same subject.
   C they didn't like their teacher.

3 Their Year 4 teacher was called
   A Mr Taylor.
   B Mr Trainor.
   C Mr Taper.

4 They didn't see each other for a few years because
   A they went to different schools.
   B Charlie was jealous of Ava.
   C they lived in different towns.

5 Charlie and Ava met again because
   A Charlie met some of Ava's friends.
   B they chose the same university course.
   C Ava went to Manchester University.

DIALOGUE

3 🔊 **6.04** **Listen to the conversation and complete the sentences with past simple verbs.**

A What ⁰___*did*___ you do in London at the weekend?

B Oh, we ¹_____ lots of things. And we ²_____ so much great food.

A I bet you ³_____ Indian food. I know it's your favourite.

B Of course! But we ⁴_____ some Chinese food, too. That ⁵_____ nice.

A Yes, it is delicious, isn't it? And I'm sure you ⁶_____ lots of things as well.

B Well, I ⁷_____ some nice clothes in the shops, but I only ⁸_____ one thing.

A And what ⁹_____ that?

B I ¹⁰_____ this belt. It's for you. I'm sorry I ¹¹_____ your birthday last week!

Train to TH!NK

Making decisions

4 You can invite a famous person to your birthday party. Who do you choose? Write the names of three people you like in the circles.

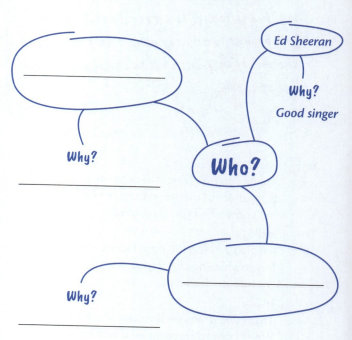

5 Next to each person write one reason for inviting him/her.

6 Use your spidergram to make a decision.

7 Write a sentence saying who you want and why.

I want to invite Ed Sheeran because he can sing for me.

A2 Key for Schools

🎧 LISTENING
Part 5: Matching

1 🔊 6.05 For each question, choose the correct answer. You will hear Kieron telling Abigail about his birthday. Which present did each person give him?

People		Presents
0 brother	C	**A** book
1 sister	☐	**B** camera
2 mum	☐	**C** DVD
3 dad	☐	**D** laptop
4 aunt	☐	**E** money
5 grandpa	☐	**F** shoes
		G tickets
		H video game

EXAM GUIDE: LISTENING PART 5

In the A2 Key for Schools Listening Part 5, there is a list of five people and a list of eight items. You listen to a dialogue and match the items to the people.

- Before listening, quickly read through the two lists.
- Remember there are three extra words in the list A–H.
- Listen carefully – don't choose an item just because you hear the word. You need to understand the meaning of the sentences it's in.
- Sometimes, you will not hear the word in the list but a similar word or a short phrase with the same meaning.

2 🔊 6.06 For each question, choose the correct answer. You will hear Christian telling his friend Charlotte about a photo of his old school friends. What clothes are his friends wearing in the photo?

People		Their clothes
0 Ella	B	**A** belt
1 Jacob	☐	**B** dress
2 Olivia	☐	**C** jacket
3 Cassie	☐	**D** jumper
4 Saffi	☐	**E** shirt
5 Adam	☐	**F** shorts
		G trainers
		H trousers

📖 READING AND WRITING
Part 7: Picture story

1 Look at the three pictures. Write the story shown in the pictures. Write 35 words or more.

EXAM GUIDE: READING AND WRITING PART 7

In A2 Key for Schools Reading and Writing Part 7, there are three pictures and you write the story you see in the pictures.

- Look at the pictures carefully before you start writing.
- Spend a few minutes thinking about the story and what you want to write.
- Decide whether to write it in the present or past tense.
- Give the people in the pictures names – it's easier.
- If you can't remember a word you need, think of another way of saying the same thing.
- Try to join some sentences together with words like: *and, so, because* … .
- Use sequencing words like: *First, then, after* … .
- Read through your story and check the spelling and grammar.

CONSOLIDATION

🎧 LISTENING

1 🔊 6.07 **Listen and tick (✓) the correct room.**

A ☐

B ☐

C ☐

2 🔊 6.07 **Listen again and answer the questions.**

1 Why does the girl like blue walls?

_____

2 Why does she like her desk under the window?

_____

3 When did she get her new wardrobe?

_____

4 Who gave her the money for the wardrobe?

_____

5 Why didn't she like her old wardrobe?

_____

6 How does her sister feel about the new wardrobe?

_____

⒢ GRAMMAR

3 **Complete the conversation with the past simple of the verbs.**

Josh I ⁰___*went*___ (go) to a party at Jack's house on Friday. It was great.

Paul Good. I'm happy that you ¹_____ (like) it. Jack's parties are good fun.

Josh Yes, they are. I ²_____ (dance) with Alice Gardner. We ³_____ (have) a great time!

Paul Yes, Alice's nice. I ⁴_____ (take) her to the cinema three weeks ago. We ⁵_____ (see) a great film.

Josh That's nice. But you ⁶_____ (not go) to Jack's party! Why not?

Paul Jack ⁷_____ (not invite) me. He ⁸_____ (have) another party two months ago, and he ⁹_____ (invite) me to that.

Josh Two months ago? I ¹⁰_____ (not know) that! Now I'm annoyed!

Paul Oh. I ¹¹_____ (say) the wrong thing. Sorry.

🄰𝗭 VOCABULARY

4 **Complete the adjectives with the missing letters.**

0 She always understands the difficult exercises. She's very i _n_ _t_ _e_ _l_ _l_ _i_ _g_ _e_ _n_ _t_ .

1 I'm sure I passed the exam. I'm very c_ _ _ _ _ _ _ _ about it.

2 The film was awful! I was really b_ _ _ _ _ .

3 I'd love to have a bedroom like yours! I'm really j_ _ _ _ _ _ _ !

4 After a long day, I like to have a long, r_ _ _ _ _ _ _ _ shower!

5 I was late with my homework again. The teacher was quite a_ _ _ _ _ _ with me.

6 He looks sad today. He usually smiles and looks c_ _ _ _ _ _ _ _ .

7 The game yesterday was great – really a_ _ _ _ _ _ _ ! I loved it.

8 She was very h_ _ _ _ _ _ and painted my room with me.

5 **Circle the correct words.**

Near our town, there's a famous old house where some rich people lived about 200 years ⁰*last* / *ago*. Last weekend, my mum said, '¹*Why* / *How* about going to visit that house?' And we did. I brought a friend of ²*my* / *mine* with us. We ³*went* / *go* by bus and my mum ⁴*paid* / *took* for us all to go in. I didn't really want to go at first because I'm usually ⁵*boring* / *bored* by museums and things. But when we got there, I thought it was ⁶*amazing* / *amazed*.

The house has got about 60 rooms and they were really ⁷*interesting* / *intelligent*. There was an enormous ⁸*sofa* / *desk* – I'm sure twenty people could sit on it! The windows were really big with beautiful red ⁹*carpets* / *curtains* on them. My dad ¹⁰*took* / *take* a photograph in one of the rooms, but a man working there got ¹¹*annoyed* / *annoying* because there was a sign that said: 'No photographs!'

DIALOGUE

6 🔊 **6.08** **Complete the conversation with the words in the list.**

about | ago | ~~bored~~ | boring | didn't | don't
enjoy | let's | sure | thought | went | why

Michael I'm so ⁰ _____bored_____ .

Jasmin How ¹_____ going for a walk?

Michael No, I ²_____ for a walk yesterday. ³_____ do something here in the house.

Jasmin A video game! ⁴_____ don't we play a video game?

Michael No. Do you remember? We played on the games console last Saturday and I ⁵_____ win a single game!

Jasmin Oh yes, I remember! I ⁶_____ it was great fun.

Michael Yes. But I didn't ⁷_____ it very much.

Jasmin Sorry, Michael. It's just a joke, OK? But here's an idea. I downloaded a film two days ⁸_____ . Why ⁹_____ we watch it now?

Michael I'm not so ¹⁰_____ . Is it one of those romantic films? They're so ¹¹_____ .

Jasmin No, don't worry. It's an action film. Come on, let's watch it.

📖 READING

7 **Read the article about making decisions. For questions 1–3, choose the correct ending, A or B.**

1 Psychologists at a university in the US wanted to find out
   A if teenagers and their friends are good car drivers.
   B what decisions teenagers make when they are with friends.

2 They noticed that teenagers behaved in a more dangerous way when
   A they thought their friends were not watching.
   B they thought their friends were watching them.

3 The experiments show that teenagers need to be careful about making decisions when
   A they are with their friends.
   B they are on their own.

✏️ WRITING

8 **Write a paragraph about you and your decisions in about 80 words. Use these questions to help you.**

- At home, what do you make decisions about? What do adults decide for you?
- Do you find it easy or difficult to make decisions? What type of decisions are easy/difficult?
- Do you ever ask for advice when making a decision?
- When you're with a group of friends, who makes the decisions? The group? You? Another person?

When teens make BAD DECISIONS

PSYCHOLOGISTS at Temple University in Philadelphia, US did an interesting experiment. They asked teenagers to play a video game that involved car driving. They could win prizes for driving fast. But the faster they drove, the bigger their risk was of losing the prize money. For half the time, the teenagers played the game on their own, and for the other half the psychologists told them that their friends were in the room next door, watching them. The results were fascinating: when the teens played the game on their own, they made much better decisions. When they thought their friends were watching, their driving was much more dangerous. They drove faster, had more accidents and often didn't stop at red lights.

Psychologists say that teens should think carefully before making important decisions when their friends are present!

7 SMART LIFE

Grammar rap!
▶20

GRAMMAR
have to / don't have to → SB p.68

1 ★☆☆ **Match the sentences with the signs.**

a

d Terminal B
Check-in desks
← B23 – B27

b

e <14 FREE for all under 14s

c

f

0 You don't have to go to Terminal A
for your flight. ☐ d
1 You have to wash your hands. ☐
2 Drivers have to turn right here. ☐
3 You have to go straight ahead. ☐
4 You have to leave your dog outside. ☐
5 Children don't have to pay. ☐

2 ★★☆ **Put the words in order to make sentences.**

0 the / a lot / have / We / Maths / study / test / to / for
We have to study a lot for the Maths test.

1 be / to / to / creative / have / find / answer / You / the
_____

2 Sundays / make / to / has / he / On / breakfast
_____

3 early / they / get / have / Do / to / up /
_____

4 Lucas / school / tomorrow / have / doesn't / to / to / go
_____

5 have / I / phone / Do / to / you /
_____

6 me / to / You / have / help / don't
_____

3 ★★☆ **Match the questions with the answers.**

0 Does your dad have to travel a lot in his job? ☐ d
1 Can I come to your place tomorrow? ☐
2 Why can't Sophie come with us to the beach? ☐
3 Does your sister live in the city centre? ☐
4 Can I go to the match on Sunday? ☐
5 Why can't I go to the cinema tonight? ☐

a I spoke to her mum. She has to help at home.
b No, she doesn't. She has to take a train every day.
c I'm afraid you can't. We have to visit Grandma.
d Yes. He goes to other countries quite a lot.
e Because you have to tidy up your room.
f No, I'm sorry. You have to study for school.

4 ★★★ **Answer the questions so they are true for you.**

1 Do you have to get up early on weekdays?
_____
_____

2 Do you have to switch off your phone at school?
_____
_____

3 Does your best friend have to help at home a lot?
_____
_____

4 Do you have to do homework over the weekend?
_____
_____

should / shouldn't → SB p.69

5 ★☆☆ **Circle the correct words.**

0 The film starts in 10 minutes. We're late, so we *should* / *shouldn't* hurry up.
1 Mum doesn't know when she'll be home, so she said we *should* / *shouldn't* wait for her to eat.
2 It's just a T-shirt. Why does it cost £65? It *should* / *shouldn't* be so expensive.
3 Why are you angry with me? You *should* / *shouldn't* try to understand me.
4 Tom needs to rest, so we *should* / *shouldn't* wake him up.
5 Juliet doesn't like her school uniform. She thinks students *should* / *shouldn't* wear what they want.

6 ★★☆ Complete the conversations. Use *should* or *shouldn't* and a phrase from the list.

> leave home earlier | ~~put on a jumper~~
> stay much longer | talk to her | worry so much

0 A I'm feeling cold.

B I think you _should put on a jumper_ .

1 A I can't believe it. I'm late for school again!

B Perhaps you _____ .

2 A I don't think Lily is very happy at all.

B Maybe you _____ .

3 A I'm a bit nervous about my English test.

B You _____ . It's not helpful.

4 A It's getting late.

B Yes, I know. We _____ .

7 ★★★ Answer the questions. Your answers can be funny or serious. Give reasons.

0 Should children get money for helping at home?

Yes, they should, because parents get money for their work, too.

1 Should students get money for going to school?

_____

2 Should the Internet be free for everybody?

_____

3 Should every child have a tablet?

_____

mustn't / don't have to   → SB p.70

8 ★☆☆ Look at the rules for a youth hostel. Circle the correct words.

HOSTEL HOUSE RULES

- Last time for checkout: 11.30 am.
- Music? OK, but use headphones.
- Switch off lights at 10 pm!
- Breakfast 7.30 – 9.30 am.
- Please wash up after eating.
- Leave your shoes near the entrance.

0 You *mustn't* / *don't have to* have the lights on after 10 pm.

1 You *mustn't* / *don't have to* leave dirty dishes in the kitchen.

2 You *mustn't* / *don't have to* play music out loud.

3 You *mustn't* / *don't have to* wear your shoes in the hostel.

4 You *mustn't* / *don't have to* check out before 10 o'clock.

5 You *mustn't* / *don't have to* have breakfast at 7.30.

9 ★★☆ Match the sentences and complete them with *mustn't* or *don't have to*.

0 My parents aren't very strict. | e |

1 Sarah hasn't got any problems with her work. | ☐ |

2 The test will be hard. | ☐ |

3 It's a secret. | ☐ |

4 The doctor says Bea's fine. | ☐ |

5 Thanks for Jamie's number. | ☐ |

a You _____ help her.

b I _____ forget to call him.

c You _____ tell anyone.

d She _____ take medicine any longer.

e I *don't have to* do much housework at home.

f You _____ forget to study every day now.

10 ★★★ Answer the questions so they are true for you.

1 What jobs do you have to do at home?

_____

_____

2 What are two things you mustn't do in your class?

_____

_____

3 Name three things you have to do during the week, but not on a Sunday.

_____

_____

4 What does your friend have to do that you don't have to do?

_____

_____

GET IT RIGHT!

have (got) to / don't have to / must / mustn't / should / shouldn't

We always use the base form of the verb after *have (got) to / don't have to / must / mustn't / should / shouldn't*.

✓ You **should ask** your sister to help you.

✗ You should ~~to~~ ask your sister to help you.

Circle the correct words.

1 You don't have *make* / *to make* / *making* dinner. We can order pizza.

2 That music is very loud. You should *use* / *to use* / *using* headphones.

3 You must *be* / *to be* / *being* careful. It's dark in the garden.

4 He shouldn't *worry* / *to worry* / *worrying* about the exam. He always gets good marks.

5 Tell Sarah she mustn't *forget* / *to forget* / *forgetting* to tidy her room.

6 What do I have *do* / *to do* / *doing* to join this club?

VOCABULARY
Gadgets

→ SB p.68

1 ★☆☆ **Complete the puzzle. What is the 'mystery word'?**

0 C O F F E E M A C H I N E

1

2

3

P

4

5

6

7

8

0 Many people need it to make a drink for the breakfast (2 words).

1 An electronic gadget that allows you to store music in a special format and play it (2 words).

2 Drivers use it to find their way.

3 You need it when your hair is wet (2 words).

4 A small light you hold in your hand; it usually has a battery.

5 A gadget or phone app that's useful for Maths.

6 The controls for a machine to play games (2 words).

7 A gadget that allows you to switch an electronic machine on or off from a distance (2 words).

8 A gadget that connects one piece of electronic equipment to another (2 words).

The mystery word is _____

Housework

→ SB p.71

2 ★☆☆ **Match the parts of the sentences.**

0 Luke's friends are staying for lunch. Can | f
1 There are no clean plates left. Can you |
2 I dropped some sugar on the floor. Will you |
3 My room is a mess, but I'm too lazy |
4 Can you do the cooking tonight? I did it |
5 I'll do the washing, but I really don't want |
6 We have no food left in the house. Can you |
7 The dishwasher's full – I have to empty it |
8 My mum showed me how to make my bed |

a do the washing up quickly?
b yesterday, and the day before yesterday.
c to tidy it.
d when I was still a child.
e do the shopping if I tell you what we need?
f you set the table, please?
g before we can load it again.
h help me vacuum it?
i to do the ironing, too.

3 ★★★ **What housework do you like/dislike? Write four sentences about you.**

I don't like ironing clothes. I think it's boring.
I don't mind doing the cooking. It's ...
I hate ... . I think it's ...

_____
_____
_____
_____
_____
_____
_____

WordWise:
Expressions with *like*

→ SB p.69

4 ★☆☆ **Match the sentences with the pictures.**

0 Abbie's like her mum. They both love nature. | c
1 It looks like a heart. |
2 I think Dad's home. That sounds like his car! |
3 It smells like an apple, but it doesn't look like one. |

a

c

b

d

REFERENCE

Gadgets	Housework		
calculator	do	load / empty	tidy up
coffee machine	the cooking	the dishwasher	the house
docking station	the ironing	vacuum	the room
games console	the shopping	the carpet	make
hair dryer	the washing	the floor	the beds
headphones	the washing-up (wash up)	set / clear	
MP3 player		the table	
remote control			
satnav			
torch			

VOCABULARY *EXTRA*

1 Write the words under the photos.

camera | keyboard | mouse | printer | screen | smartwatch

0

camera

1

_____

2

_____

3

_____

4

_____

5

_____

2 Complete the lists.

1 Electronic gadgets your family has at home: _____

2 The five gadgets you use most: _____

GADGETS FOR A BETTER WORLD

Professor Joshua Silver is a physicist at the University of Oxford. He also can't see very well! Joshua doesn't like buying new glasses when his eyes get worse. He had an idea to make glasses where you can change the strength of the lens. The glasses have liquid inside the plastic. To make the glasses stronger, you turn a wheel on each lens and this adds more liquid. If the glasses are too strong, you turn the wheel the other way, taking away some of the liquid. The liquid changes the shape of the lens. It's an incredibly useful invention, and it is also very cheap to make each pair of glasses.

Glasses that anyone can use, and that last forever, have the power to change people's lives. Joshua Silver is working to provide 1 billion pairs of his glasses to people around the world. This means that children can read their lessons at school and adults can continue to work and support their families.

Kenneth Shinozuka from New York City, US, lives with his parents and grandparents. Kenneth's grandfather has Alzheimer's, a disease that is common in old people. People with this illness often forget things and sometimes get lost. Kenneth's grandfather kept getting out of bed at night and walking around. One night, he left the house and his family were very worried because they didn't know where he was.

Kenneth wanted to do something to help his grandpa. What was his idea? A brilliant invention called SafeWander. Small discs go on the bottom of a normal pair of socks. When the person steps on the floor, the discs send a message to a smartphone and the phone rings an alarm. Kenneth tested the socks on his grandfather and they worked! Now his family don't have to watch Grandpa all night. He wears the socks and they know when he gets out of bed. Kenneth was only 15 when he made SafeWander and he won prizes for his invention. Now his 'smart socks' are helping other people like his grandfather to stay safe.

🔍 8   ♡ 16   🔁 5

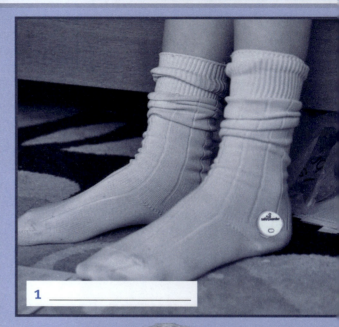
1 _____

2 _____

📖 READING

1 **Read the article. Write the names of the inventors under the photos.**

2 **Read the article again. Mark the sentences T (true) or F (false). Correct the false sentences.**

   0 Joshua Silver needs glasses.   `T`

   1 With Joshua's glasses, people only need one pair. ☐

   2 He has sold a billion pairs of glasses. ☐

   3 Kenneth doesn't spend much time with his grandfather. ☐

   4 Kenneth's grandfather often got lost during the day. ☐

   5 Kenneth's invention helps people with Alzheimer's. ☐

3 **CRITICAL THINKING** **Which of the gadgets in the article is the most useful? Why?**

_____

_____

_____

4 **CRITICAL THINKING** **Complete the table with three gadgets that you use.**

Name of gadget	What it helps you to do

DEVELOPING Writing

Taking notes and writing a short paragraph

1 INPUT Read the text. Tick (✓) the things that Alexander Graham Bell experimented with.

Home About Latest news

A famous INVENTOR

When Alexander Graham Bell was 29, he made one of the most important inventions in the history of the world: the telephone. A year later, he started the Bell Telephone Company. It became very successful. He became a businessman and earned a lot of money from his telephone company.

But Alexander Graham Bell wasn't only interested in money. He was interested in making inventions. He always wanted to learn and to try and create new things. He never stopped thinking of new ideas. He used his money to open laboratories with teams of engineers who could help him make his dreams come true.

Bell was also fascinated with propellers and kites and did lots of experiments with them. In 1907, four years after the Wright Brothers made their first flight, Bell formed the Aerial Experiment Association with four young engineers. Their plan was to build planes. The group was successful. Their plane named Silver Dart made the first successful flight in Canada on 23 February 1909.

 1

 2

 3

 4

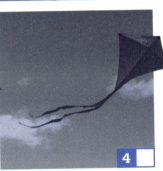 5

2 ANALYSE Look at a student's notes on the first paragraph of the text in Exercise 1. Underline the ideas in the text that the student used.

Alexander Graham Bell

1 29: invented telephone
2 30: started Bell Telephone Company — very successful
3 businessman — lots of money

3 PLAN Read the second and third paragraphs of the text again. Underline five important points and write them in the form of notes.

_____
_____
_____
_____
_____

✎ WRITING TIP: making notes on a text

- Read the whole text for general understanding.
- Read each paragraph carefully and underline the important information.
- For each paragraph make short notes: just write words, not sentences, and leave out all unnecessary information.
- Make sure your notes are clear and include all the important information from each paragraph.

4 PRODUCE Write a paragraph to summarise the text about Alexander Graham Bell in 100–130 words using your notes from Exercises 2 and 3.

LISTENING

1 🔊 **7.01** Listen to the conversations. For questions 1–3, choose the correct answers A, B or C.

Conversation 1

1 What's the problem?

   A The camera doesn't work.

   B The USB cable isn't plugged in.

   C The laptop doesn't work.

Conversation 2

2 What does Daniel have to do?

   A tidy his room

   B walk the dog

   C wash up

Conversation 3

3 What did Evan borrow without asking?

   A a digital camera

   B an MP3 player

   C a laptop

2 🔊 **7.01** Listen again. Complete the sentences from the conversations.

Stella	Let ⁰ _me_ ¹s_____ . You ²h_____ ³t_____ switch ⁴y_____ ⁵c_____ on.
Daniel	All right. ⁶G_____ you. Do I ⁷h_____ to ⁸t_____ up my desk ⁹t_____ ?
Lily	Well, you ¹⁰m_____ use ¹¹m_____ ¹²th_____ without ¹³a_____ .

DIALOGUE

3 🔊 **7.02** Complete the conversation with the expressions in the list.

> do you mean | like what | sorry

Oliver	I want to do a mini-triathlon on Sunday.
Maya	¹_____ ?
Oliver	A mini-triathlon. That's three races in one.
Maya	Three races in one? What ²_____ ?
Oliver	Well, you have to swim 1 km, cycle 10 km, and run 3 km.
Maya	Really? That sounds like hard work. Why is it called mini?
Oliver	Because in a normal triathlon there are harder challenges.
Maya	³_____ ?
Oliver	Well, in the Olympic triathlon they swim 1.5 km, cycle 40 km, and run 10 km.
Maya	Wow! I think we should try the mini race!
Oliver	I think you're right.

4 Write a short conversation for this picture. Use some of the expressions from Exercises 2 and 3.

_____

_____

_____

_____

_____

_____

_____

_____

PHRASES FOR FLUENCY ↪ SB p.72

5 🔊 **7.03** Complete the conversation with the expressions in the list.

> absolutely | all right | and stuff
> ~~Hey~~ | never mind | no chance

Ada	⁰_____ _Hey_ _____ , Esma, what are you doing after school?
Esma	After school? Why?
Ada	I just want to know if you want to play basketball.
Esma	Basketball! ¹_____ , I've got to do housework ²_____ .
Ada	OK, ³_____ . So, what about tomorrow? Can we play then?
Esma	⁴_____ .
Ada	⁵_____ , see you then. Don't forget your basketball things!

> **PRONUNCIATION**
> Vowel sounds: /ʊ/ and /uː/ Go to page 120.

A2 Key for Schools

1 For each question, choose the correct answer.

1

Please turn off the coffee machine at night and keep this area clean.

What is this sign telling people to do?

A They must clean the coffee machine every night.

B They should turn off the coffee machine before they clean it.

C They must not leave the machine on during the night.

2

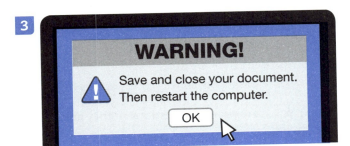

14:10

Hanna,
Can you take Tommy to his piano lesson this afternoon?
You don't have to take the dog out, Lewis can do it today.
Dad

A Hanna must take the dog for a walk.

B Hanna must ask Lewis to collect Tommy.

C Hanna has to go with Tommy to his lesson.

3

WARNING!

⚠ Save and close your document. Then restart the computer.

OK

A There is no problem with the computer.

B You should switch off and then switch on.

C You don't have to save your work.

4

No digital gadgets in the exam room.

PLEASE LEAVE HERE.

A Students don't have to take their phones into the room.

B Students mustn't take their phones into the room.

C Students can't leave their phones here.

5

WARNING!

This toy has small parts. It is dangerous and **not** for children under 3.

A Children under three must be careful with this toy.

B This toy is for small children.

C Only children over three should use this toy.

6

Joe,
I'll be home late today, I'm going to an art class after work.
Please start making dinner, but don't eat without me!
Mum

A Mum will be back at the usual time.

B Joe must wait for his mum.

C Joe doesn't have to cook dinner.

EXAM GUIDE: READING AND WRITING PART 1

In A2 Key for Schools Reading and Writing Part 1, there are six short texts and you choose the option with the correct meaning. The texts are usually notices, signs, emails or text messages. There are three options and you choose one.

- Look at the context: Is it a message? A notice? Where would you see it?
- You won't always find the same words in the texts and sentences. Look for words and phrases with similar meanings.
- Often the sentences summarise the whole text but say it in a different way.
- Be careful when there are negative verbs.
- When you finish, read through your answers again to check they are right.

8 A QUESTION OF SPORT

Grammar rap!
▶23

GRAMMAR
Past continuous
→ SB p.76

1 ★☆☆ **Complete the text with *was* or *were*.**

It was a cold winter's morning. It ⁰_____ *was* _____ raining a little. Mums and dads ¹_____ standing by the school football field. They ²_____ chatting and drinking coffee to keep warm. They ³_____ waiting for the game to begin.

On the field, their daughters ⁴_____ getting ready for the big match. Some of them ⁵_____ running and others ⁶_____ kicking balls about. The goalkeeper ⁷_____ practising catching the ball.

Everyone was excited. It was the final of the under 16s girls' football tournament. Mr Fletcher, the headmaster, ⁸_____ cleaning his glasses. He put them on, took the whistle out of his pocket, and blew it.

2 ★★★ **Complete the text. Choose the correct words and write them in the correct form.**

clap | cry | hold | ~~jump~~ | not enjoy
not feel | sit | take | talk

I got there very late. The game was over. The girls of Blacon High School ⁰_____ *were jumping* _____ up and down. They were the champions. Their proud parents ¹_____ .
One girl ²_____ up the trophy and showing it to the crowd and a journalist ³_____ lots of photos.
But not everyone was happy. The girls on the losing team ⁴_____ on the ground.
Some of them had their heads in their hands and they ⁵_____ . They certainly ⁶_____ the celebrations.
Mr Fletcher ⁷_____ to them, but they ⁸_____ great.
Another year and still no trophy.

PRONUNCIATION
Strong and weak forms of *was* and *were*
Go to page 120. 🎧

3 ★★☆ **Complete the sentences. Use the past continuous of the verbs in brackets.**

0 Phoebe _____ *wasn't watching* _____ (not watch) TV, she _____ *was playing* _____ (play) games.

1 I _____ (not play) tennis, I _____ (watch) a tennis match.

2 They _____ (not speak) Polish, they _____ (speak) Russian.

3 Our team _____ (not lose), we _____ (win).

4 Dad _____ (not swim), he _____ (sit) on the beach.

4 ★☆☆ **Match the questions with the answers.**

0 Were you listening to me? [d]
1 Was he laughing? ☐
2 Was it raining? ☐
3 Were they talking? ☐
4 Was I sleeping? ☐
5 Were we making a lot of noise? ☐

a Yes, it was. We got really wet.
b Yes, they were, but I didn't hear what they said.
c Yes, I think you were.
d Yes, I heard everything you said.
e No, I don't think we were.
f No, he wasn't. He didn't think it was very funny.

5 ★★☆ **Answer the questions so they are true for you.**

What were you doing …

1 at 7 am today?
_____

2 at 6 pm yesterday?
_____

3 this time yesterday?
_____

4 at 10 o'clock last Sunday morning?
_____

Past continuous vs. past simple →SB p.79

6 ★☆☆ **Match the parts of the sentences.**

0 While the teacher was talking, [e]
1 Evan was making an omelette ☐
2 The boys were fighting ☐
3 We were staying in a youth hostel ☐
4 While I was reading in the bath, ☐
5 She was brushing her teeth ☐

a when he burned his hand on the pan.
b when their mum walked into the room.
c I dropped my book in the water.
d but the toothbrush broke.
e I put my hand up to ask a question.
f when we met Sandro.

7 ★★☆ **Circle the correct words.**

0 Matthew *played* / *(was playing)* the guitar when he *(fell)* / *was falling* off the stage.
1 I *watched* / *was watching* a football match when my sister *came* / *was coming* into the room.
2 John and his sister *walked* / *were walking* to school when the accident *happened* / *was happening*.
3 I *talked* / *was talking* about Kiki when she *phoned* / *was phoning* me.
4 Alma *fell* / *was falling* and hurt her leg while she *skied* / *was skiing*.
5 While Ellie *studied* / *was studying*, she *remembered* / *was remembering* it was her mum's birthday.
6 Josh *lost* / *was losing* his phone while he *ran* / *was running*.

when and *while* →SB p.79

8 ★★☆ **Complete the sentences with *when* or *while*.**

0 ___*While*___ I was trying to get to sleep, the dog started barking.
1 She was eating an apple _____ she bit her tongue.
2 We were driving in the car _____ we saw Robin on his bike.
3 _____ I was waiting at the bus stop, I realised I didn't have any money.
4 Olivia was doing the Maths test _____ her phone rang.
5 _____ I was walking into town, I saw I had different socks on.

9 ★★★ **Write two sentences about each picture.**

0 Pablo / swim / saw / a turtle

While Pablo was swimming, he saw a turtle.
Pablo was swimming when he saw a turtle.

1 George / rock climb / drop / his bag

_____
_____

2 Megan / windsurf / fall / into the sea

_____
_____

3 Sasha and Eva / walk / in the mountains / they / got lost

_____
_____

GET IT RIGHT!

Past continuous

We form the past continuous with *was*/*were* + the *-ing* form of the verb. We use *was* with *I*, *he* and *she* and *were* with *we*, *you* and *they*.

✓ We were playing football when it started to rain.
✗ We ~~was playing~~ football when it started to rain.
✓ I was windsurfing when the accident happened.
✗ I ~~were windsurfing~~ when the accident happened.

Complete the sentences with *was* or *were*.

1 The rain started while they _____ having a picnic.
2 My friends and I _____ enjoying the competition when the TV stopped working.
3 My brother _____ winning the race when he fell off his bike.
4 _____ you driving when it started to snow?

VOCABULARY
Sports and sports verbs

→ SB p.76

1 ★★☆ Use the photos to find nine sports that fit into the word lines. The grey boxes contain the last letter of one word and the first letter of the next word.

					S											
				G								S				
			S					G		F						

There are four sports that don't fit into the word lines. What are they?

1 _____ 2 _____ 3 _____ 4 _____

2 ★★★ Circle the odd word out and explain why.

0 tennis   rugby   windsurfing   basketball
The other sports all use balls.

1 skiing   snowboarding   swimming   ski jumping
_____

2 windsurfing   rock climbing   sailing   diving
_____

3 tennis   rugby   volleyball   football
_____

Adverbs of sequence

→ SB p.79

3 ★★☆ Write sentences. Use the expressions in the list to start each sentence.

> At first | After half an hour | Finally | Then

0 nervous
At first, I was nervous.

1 instructor / show / what to do
_____

2 could stand up
_____

3 ski / down the hill
_____

4 ★★★ Write a mini-story. Use the expressions and your own ideas.

<u>The Tennis Game</u>

1 At first …
2 Then …
3 After …
4 Finally …

REFERENCE
Sports

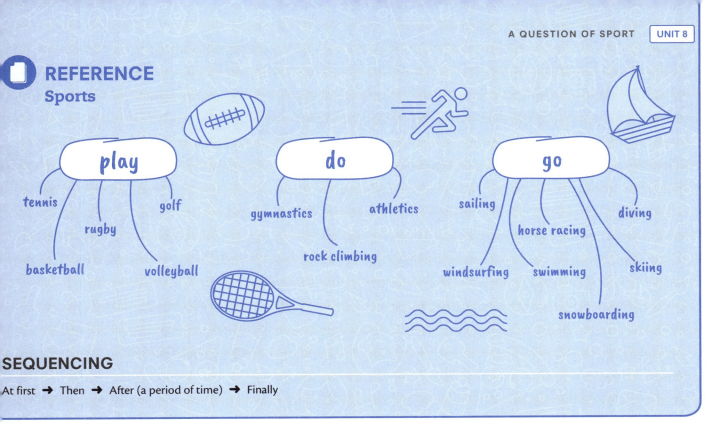

play
tennis
rugby
golf
basketball
volleyball

do
gymnastics
athletics
rock climbing

go
sailing
diving
horse racing
windsurfing
swimming
skiing
snowboarding

SEQUENCING

At first ➔ Then ➔ After (a period of time) ➔ Finally

VOCABULARY *EXTRA*

1 Write the words under the pictures.

> badminton | baseball | ~~hockey~~
> inline skating | surfing | table tennis

2 Complete the mind map with the names of sports.

0

hockey

1

2

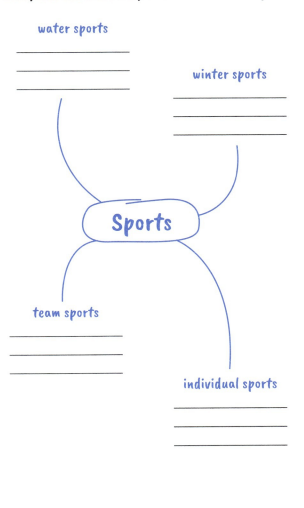

3

4

5

water sports
_____
_____
_____

winter sports
_____
_____
_____

Sports

team sports
_____
_____
_____

individual sports
_____
_____
_____

People who changed sport:
DICK FOSBURY

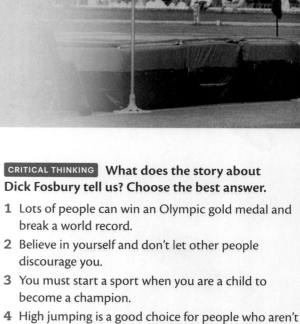

1

2

3

Like many American teenagers, Dick Fosbury wanted to be a professional sportsman, but he had a problem – he wasn't very good at any sport. He didn't play football well, and although he was tall, he wasn't a very good basketball player either. When he tried athletics, his results still weren't great, but he found that he had some talent for the high jump.

At that time, there were two popular styles of jumping over the bar. There was *the scissors*, where the athlete lifted one leg first and then the other over the bar, and there was *the straddle*, where the athlete went over the bar in a lying position, face down. Fosbury used the straddle. The best height he could jump was 1.63 m. It wasn't bad, but it was a long way from the Olympic record of 2.23 m.

One afternoon, Fosbury decided to do something completely different. He took off backwards and jumped over the bar on his back, face up. The results were amazing. That day he improved his personal best by 15 cm. In the following years, he spent all his time practising, getting better and better. He was starting to win competitions, but most people were confused by his strange style. A year before the 1968 Olympics, he was the number 61 jumper in the world, and he was lucky to get into the US Olympic team.

When he arrived in Mexico, not many people knew his name. On the day of the high jump final, he walked on to the field with all the other jumpers. As the competition started, the 80,000 people in the crowd began to notice that one of the jumpers had a very strange style. At first they thought it was funny and laughed each time Fosbury jumped over the bar. After nearly four hours there were only three jumpers left. The crowd weren't laughing at Fosbury any more – they were cheering him on. The bar was at 2.24 m – a new Olympic record. The other two jumpers knocked it off but Fosbury flew over. The gold medal was his.

Dick Fosbury was now famous all over the world and his *Fosbury flop* changed forever the way that high jumpers jumped.

READING

1 **Read the article. Match photos 1–3 with the names of the high jump styles in *italics*.**

2 **Read the article again. Answer the questions.**

   0 Why did Fosbury choose to do the high jump?
   Because it was the only sport that he was good at.

   1 How high could he jump on the day he invented his new style?
   _____

   2 What did people first think about his new style?
   _____

   3 How good was he at the high jump in 1967?
   _____

   4 Was he the favourite to win the gold medal in the Olympics? Explain your answer.
   _____

   5 How do people remember Dick Fosbury today?
   _____

3 **CRITICAL THINKING** **What does the story about Dick Fosbury tell us? Choose the best answer.**

   1 Lots of people can win an Olympic gold medal and break a world record.

   2 Believe in yourself and don't let other people discourage you.

   3 You must start a sport when you are a child to become a champion.

   4 High jumping is a good choice for people who aren't very good at sport.

4 **CRITICAL THINKING** **Why do you think Dick Fosbury was successful? Put the ideas in order of importance for you.**

   ☐ He wanted to be a sports champion.
   ☐ His new way of jumping was very good.
   ☐ He trained and practised a lot.
   ☐ He didn't worry when people laughed at him.

DEVELOPING Writing

An article

1 **INPUT** **Read the text. Where do you think it comes from?**

A A newspaper ☐   **B** A school magazine ☐   **C** A holiday website ☐   **D** A story book ☐

How I got into MOUNTAIN BIKING

By Caitlin Rogers

It was all because of my best friend, Zara. We were having lunch one day when ¹☐. I didn't have my own bike at that time, but Zara lent me her old one. We went to a forest that she knew very well and we got on our bikes. I was soon riding up and down the hills and it felt great! And guess what? ²☐. It's the same as riding a normal bike – you are just riding on paths instead of on the road.

I asked for a bike for my birthday ³☐. Now I ride every weekend. Sometimes we get a little wet and dirty, but I don't mind. ⁴☐. So, if you like doing exercise and being outside, maybe mountain biking is for you, too!

2 **ANALYSE** **Read the text again and complete it with the missing sentences. Write A–D in the gaps.**

A It's all part of the fun

B You don't have to go fast

C and then I joined the local club

D she invited me to go mountain biking with her

✏ WRITING TIP: an article

An article is a piece of writing in a newspaper, magazine or on a website.

- Think about your readers. Who are they? What are they interested in?
- You can use informal language in an article.
- You can speak to the readers directly. For example, you might want to ask a question or make a suggestion.
- Don't just write about facts. Describe what the experience was like and how you felt.
- Use some adjectives and adverbs to make your writing interesting.

3 **PLAN** **Choose ONE of these topics for an article and make notes in the plan.**

- A sports match between your school and another one
- A school trip
- How you started a new sport

TITLE: _____

PARAGRAPH 1: Set up the situation (e.g. time, place).

_____

_____

PARAGRAPH 2: Describe what happened.

_____

_____

PARAGRAPH 3: Describe how the situation ended and/or give your opinion.

_____

_____

4 **PRODUCE** **Write your article for a school magazine (about 120–140 words). Use your notes from Exercise 3.**

🎧 LISTENING

1 🔊 **8.02** Listen to the street interviews. Who does, or wants to do, these sports, the girl (G) or the boy (B)?

 **0** G    **3** ☐    **6** ☐

 **1** ☐    **4** ☐    **7** ☐

 **2** ☐    **5** ☐    **8** ☐

2 🔊 **8.02** Listen again. Mark the sentences T (true) or F (false).

0 The girl thinks the sports centre looks good. ☐ T
1 The girl isn't very interested in sport. ☐
2 You can do water sports at the sports centre. ☐
3 The boy thinks the sports centre cost too much. ☐
4 The sports centre has a skating track. ☐

DIALOGUE

3 Put the words in order to make questions and answers.

0 of / sports / do / think / What / centre? / you / the / new
   What do you think of the new sports centre?

1 brilliant / think / I / it's
   _____

2 sports / do / feel / you / centre? / How / the / about / new
   _____

3 money / of / I / a / waste / it's / think
   _____

4 🔊 **8.03** Put the sentences in order to make a conversation.

A ☐ Well, we need a new swimming pool.
A ☐ I don't agree.
A ☐1 What do you think of the new library?
A ☐ I think it's a waste of money. There are better things to spend our money on.
B ☐ For example?
B ☐ I like it. I think it's really good for our town.
B ☐ So how do you feel about it, then?
B ☐ I'm sorry, but I think a library is more important than a swimming pool.

Train to TH!NK

Sequencing

5 Which sequence (A–E) do these words belong to and where should they go?

0 afternoon ☐C *between morning and evening*
1 baby ☐ _____
2 today ☐ _____
3 Saturday ☐ _____
4 wake up ☐ _____

A	child teenager adult
B	Monday Wednesday Friday
C	morning evening night
D	go to school have lunch come home
E	yesterday tomorrow next weekend

6 Put the lists of words in order. Add one more item at the end of each list.

0 October / March / June
   March, June, October, (November)

1 third / second / fourth
   _____

2 get into the water / go to the sports centre / go to the pool
   _____

3 sometimes / often / rarely
   _____

A2 Key for Schools

🎧 LISTENING
Part 2: Gap fill

1 🔊 **8.04** **For each question, write the correct answer in the gap. Write one word, or a number, or a date or a time.**

You will hear a girl talking about her football team.

Name: Boxton United Girls' Football Club
Training day: [1]_____
Kit: Yellow shirt and [2]_____ shorts
Cost: [3]_____ a month
Training: at the park in [4]_____ Road
Contact Becky on: [5]_____

EXAM GUIDE: LISTENING PART 2

In A2 Key for Schools Listening Part 2, you listen to one person speaking and complete some notes.

- Before you listen, read the title and the notes carefully because they give you an idea about what you are going to hear.
- Focus on the gaps and try to imagine what sort of information you need to listen for – for example, a date, a price, a number or a word.
- You will hear the missing information in the same order as the notes.
- Use the first listening to write in as many of the answers as you can. Use the second listening to check these answers and complete the other gaps.

2 🔊 **8.05** **For each question, write the correct answer in each gap. Write one word, or a number, or a date or a time. You will hear a boy talking about the Olympic Stadium in Rio de Janeiro.**

- Name: The Maracanã Stadium
- Distance from Copacabana beach: [1]_____ km
- Opened in [2]_____ 1950
- The 1950 FIFA World Cup winners were: [3]_____
- The Olympic and Paralympic games took place here in [4]_____
- Stadium used for: football and [5]_____

🎧 LISTENING
Part 4: 3-option multiple choice

EXAM GUIDE: LISTENING PART 4

In A2 Key for Schools Listening Part 4, you listen to five short dialogues and monologues and then choose the correct answer A, B or C.

- Before you listen, read the questions and the three options.
- You hear each dialogue or monologue twice.
- The questions are not usually about details or facts. You need to identify the main point, idea, message or the gist of what you hear.
- When you listen, focus on general understanding and listen for key words.
- Don't choose an answer just because you hear the same word in the listening. Listen carefully to what the speakers say about it.

3 🔊 **8.06** **For each question, choose the correct answer.**

1 You will hear two friends talking about a football match. Why does the boy feel upset?
   A They played badly.
   B His team were lucky.
   C They lost the match.

2 You will hear a sports teacher giving instructions to her class. Which sport are they playing?
   A basketball
   B tennis
   C football

3 You will hear a sports report on the radio. Which country won the competition?
   A Australia
   B the US
   C Canada

4 You will hear two friends talking. Where did the accident happen?
   A in the mountains
   B in the hotel
   C in a ski lesson

5 You will hear two friends talking about a competition. How does Ellie feel?
   A happy
   B sad
   C worried

CONSOLIDATION

🎧 LISTENING

1 🔊 **8.07** **Listen to the conversation. Choose the correct answer A, B or C.**

1 What lesson has Lucy got at the sports centre today?
- **A** gym
- **B** rock climbing
- **C** swimming

2 What is in the bathroom?
- **A** a hair dryer
- **B** a tablet
- **C** headphones

3 What is on the living room floor?
- **A** magazines
- **B** a games console
- **C** a docking station

2 🔊 **8.07** **Listen again and answer the questions.**

0 How long is it until Lucy's lesson starts?
Two hours.

1 Why does she want to go to the sports centre early?
_____
_____

2 What does her dad want her to do?
_____
_____

3 What was Lucy's dad doing when he sat on the headphones?
_____
_____

4 Where is Lucy's tablet?
_____
_____

5 Where does Lucy's dad want her to help him?
_____
_____

6 Why does he think cutting wood is a good idea for Lucy?
_____
_____

🇦z VOCABULARY

3 **Unscramble the letters and write the words.**

0 I'd love to go *nagilis*, but I can't swim and I'm scared I might fall in the water. _____sailing_____

1 We don't all want to listen to your music. Put your *oehadpenhs* on. _____

2 I can't do this sum. Can I use the *alaclutocr* on your phone? _____

3 I tried to play *fogl* once, but I couldn't even hit the ball. _____

4 It's dark. I can't see anything. Have you got a *corth*? _____

Ⓖ GRAMMAR

4 **Complete the sentences with the correct form of the verbs.**

0 They ____had____ (have) the accident while they __were programming__ (program) the satnav.

1 I _____ (tidy) up my bedroom when I _____ (find) my torch.

2 She _____ (use) the coffee maker when she _____ (burn) her hand.

3 Dad _____ (tell) us to do our homework when we _____ (play) on the games console.

4 I _____ (listen) to music on my phone when it _____ (stop) working.

5 Ⓒircle the correct words.

Dad Hey, Max, why are you looking so sad?

Max We lost the match.

Dad You ⁰(shouldn't)/ *must* worry so much. You ¹*mustn't always / don't always* have to win.

Max Yes, but we never win. We ²*should / don't have to* try to win sometimes. Our coach says we ³*shouldn't / must* try harder. He thinks we ⁴*should / mustn't* have extra training sessions.

Dad What! You already have three. I think I ⁵*should / mustn't* have a chat with him.

Max It's OK, Dad. You ⁶*mustn't / don't have to* do that. I don't think I want to play for the team any more.

Dad Come on, Max, you ⁷*shouldn't / must* give up so easily.

Max But you always say that we ⁸*should / don't have to* love what we do. I don't even like playing football.

Dad Well, you ⁹*must / shouldn't* always listen to what I say. Sometimes even I get it wrong.

DIALOGUE

6 🔊 8.08 **Complete the conversation with the words in the list.**

> doing | fear | mean | ~~should~~ | skiing | sorry | sport | tell | what | windsurfing

Amy I'm bored.

Leo You ⁰_____should_____ get a hobby, then.

Amy Like ¹_____ ?

Leo Well, maybe you could start doing a
² _____ .

Amy You ³_____ do some exercise?

Leo Exactly. What about a water sport? Sailing or
⁴_____ , or something like that.

Amy But I've got aquaphobia – you know, a fear of water.

Leo OK, what about rock climbing? They do lessons at the gym.

Amy No, I've got acrophobia.

Leo ⁵_____ ?

Amy Acrophobia – it's a ⁶_____ of heights.

Leo Snowboarding? ⁷_____ ?

Amy No, I've got chionophobia.

Leo Don't ⁸_____ me – a fear of snow.

Amy Exactly.

Leo I think you've got lazyitis.

Amy What's that?

Leo The fear of ⁹_____ exercise!

📖 READING

7 **Read the text. Match the headings with the paragraphs.**

0 The prizes ☑ C

1 The places ☐

2 Try saying this! ☐

3 Young and old ☐

✏️ WRITING

8 **Choose a sport or a sportsperson that you like. Write a text called 'All you need to know about … ' (about 150 words).**

- Research some interesting facts and trivia.
- Organise your text into three or four short paragraphs.
- Try to write exactly 150 words.

ALL YOU NEED TO KNOW ABOUT THE
OLYMPIC GAMES IN 150 WORDS

A London is the only city to hold the Games three times (in 1908, 1948 and 2012). The US held them four times but in three different cities.

B At the Paris Games in 1900, there were more athletes than spectators. The oldest athlete ever at the games was Sweden's Oscar Swahn. He won a silver medal in shooting in 1920 at the age of 72. The youngest medal winner was Inge Sorensen from Denmark. She was 12 when she won a bronze medal in swimming.

C In the first modern Olympic Games, in Athens in 1896, there were no gold medals. The winners all got silver medals. In the 1900 Games, the winners got trophies instead of medals. Winners first got gold medals in the 1904 Olympics in St Louis, US.

D And finally, the longest name for an Olympic champion was Prapawadee Jaroenrattanatarakoon from Thailand. She won a gold medal in weightlifting.

9 WILD AND WONDERFUL

Grammar rap!

▶26

GRAMMAR
Comparative adjectives → SB p.86

1 ★☆☆ **Write the comparative form of the adjectives.**

0 old ___older___

1 bad _____

2 beautiful _____

3 easy _____

4 expensive _____

5 good _____

6 happy _____

7 interesting _____

8 nice _____

9 young _____

2 ★★☆ **Complete sentence B with the comparative form of the adjective in A.**

0 A Question number 1 is difficult.

B Yes, it is – but question number 2 is _____more difficult_____ !

1 A Was your laptop expensive?

B Yes, it was, but the old one was _____ .

2 A She's young.

B Yes, but her sister's _____ than her.

3 A This book's interesting.

B You're right, but the other one is _____ .

4 A Wow – that's a good bike!

B It's not bad. Actually, I want to buy a _____ one than this!

5 A This film's bad!

B Yes, but the other one was _____ !

3 ★★☆ **Complete the sentences. Use the comparative form of the adjectives.**

	Siena	Justine
Age:	12	13
Height:	1.58	1.56
Does homework:	sometimes	always
English score:	93%	74%

0 Siena is ___younger than___ Justine. (young)

1 Siena is _____ Justine. (tall)

2 Justine is _____ Siena. (hard-working)

3 Siena is _____ at English _____ Justine. (good)

4 ★★★ **Write comparative sentences using your own ideas. Use the words in brackets to help you.**

1 your school / another school in your town (*big / good …?*)

_____

2 you / your best friend (*old / tall / intelligent …?*)

_____

3 two video games (*easy / enjoyable / exciting …?*)

_____

4 (any two things you want to compare)

_____

can / can't for ability → SB p.87

5 ★☆☆ **Complete the sentences. Use *can* or *can't*.**

0 She ___can ride.___

2 She _____

1 He _____

3 He _____

6 ★★☆ **Complete the sentences using *can ... but ... can't ....* Think about sports, languages, music, cooking, art, etc.**

0 I ___can sing, but I can't play any instruments.___

1 My best friend _____

2 My mum / dad _____

3 Babies _____

4 Dogs _____

5 I _____

Superlative adjectives

→ SB p.88

7 ★☆☆ **Complete the conversations.**

> the best | ~~the laziest~~ | the most difficult
> the most expensive | the most interesting
> the oldest | the worst

0 A Who's _____the laziest_____ kid in your class?

  B Yuri. He never does anything!

1 A That test was hard!

  B It was. In fact it was _____
  test this year.

2 A Do you think they're a good band?

  B Yes, I do. They're _____ band
  around at the moment.

3 A That's a great shirt.

  B Yes, it's really nice. But I can't buy it.
  It's _____ shirt in the shop!

4 A What a horrible day. Rain, rain, rain.

  B Yes, I think it's _____ day of
  the summer.

5 A Who's _____ person in your
  family?

  B Grandpa. He's 74.

6 A You really like History, don't you?

  B Yes, I think it's _____ subject
  at school.

8 ★★☆ **Complete the sentences with the
superlative form of the adjectives in the list.**

> boring | delicious | fast | high
> important | ~~rich~~ | strong

0 She's got a really big house and a Porsche.
She's ____the richest____ person I know!

1 He can pick up a 50 kilo bag of potatoes.
He's _____ man I know.

2 I almost fell asleep during the film.
It was _____ film ever!

3 Let's have an ice cream here. It's _____
ice cream in town!

4 This car does 280 kph. Maybe it's _____
car in the world.

5 Which is _____ mountain in the world?

6 Some people say that the day you get married is
_____ day of your life.

9 ★★☆ Circle **the correct words.**

0 Is the Amazon *longer* / *the longest* river in the world?

1 Alex is *taller* / *the tallest* than me.

2 Yesterday was *colder* / *the coldest* day of the year.

3 My father is *younger* / *the youngest* than my mother.

4 He wants to be *richer* / *the richest* person in the
country.

5 Is this exercise *easier* / *the easiest* one on this page?

10 ★★★ **Write one comparative sentence and
one superlative sentence about the things in each
group. Use the adjectives in the list to help you.**

> big | boring | cheap | ~~cold~~ | delicious,
> difficult | enjoyable | fast | good | healthy
> ~~hot~~ | interesting

0 winter – summer – autumn
Summer is hotter than autumn.
Winter's the coldest time of the year.

1 running – football – swimming
_____
_____

2 pizza – chips – salad
_____
_____

3 video games – films – books
_____
_____

4 Brazil – China – Britain
_____
_____

5 train – plane – bus
_____
_____

GET IT RIGHT!

Comparative and superlative adjectives

We form the comparative of <u>long</u> adjectives with
more + adjective. We form the comparative of <u>short</u>
adjectives (one syllable) with adjective + *-er*. Don't
use *more* with adjective + *-er*.

✓ My cousin is **younger** than me.

✗ My cousin is ~~more younger~~ than me.

We form the superlative of long adjectives with *the
most* + adjective. We form the superlative of short
adjectives (one syllable) with *the* + adjective + *-est*.
Don't use *the most* with short adjective + *-est*.

✓ It was **the coldest** winter in history.

✗ It was the ~~most coldest~~ winter in history.

**Complete the text with the comparative or
superlative form of the adjectives in brackets.**

I love climbing mountains. For me, it's [1]_____
(exciting) hobby. I think [2]_____ (beautiful)
mountains in the world are in New Zealand. But
[3]_____ (tall) mountains in the world are in
Asia. The mountains in Britain are [4]_____
(low) than in Asia and the weather is [5]_____
(wet). The US has [6]_____ (warm) weather than
Britain, but Asia's weather is [7]_____ (hot).
So I love going climbing in Asia.

VOCABULARY

Geographical features → SB p.86

1 ★★☆ **Match the words a–j with the definitions 1–9.**

0 a place with lots of trees growing together — *a*

1 an area of sand or rocks near the sea ☐

2 land with water all round it ☐

3 high land but not as high as a mountain ☐

4 water that moves across the land and into the sea ☐

5 very high land, sometimes with snow on top ☐

6 a big area of water with land around it ☐

7 a very large area of sea water ☐

8 a hot, humid forest with lots of tropical plants and animals ☐

9 a big, hot, dry area of land, often with sand ☐

a forest **f** jungle
b island **g** ocean
c hill **h** river
d desert **i** lake
e beach **j** mountain

2 ★★★ **Complete the sentences with the words in Exercise 1.**

0 It's important to take lots of water with you if you go into the ___*desert*___ .

1 Madagascar is a very big _____ in the Indian Ocean.

2 I love sitting on a _____ and swimming in the sea.

3 The longest _____ in the world is the Nile.

4 Mount Everest is the highest _____ in the world.

5 I was very tired after I cycled up the _____ .

6 Let's go for a walk in the _____ and look for wild mushrooms!

7 We sailed round the _____ in a small boat.

8 Tigers live in the _____ in India and Indonesia.

9 The ship hit a rock and went to the bottom of the _____ .

The weather → SB p.89

3 ★☆☆ **Complete the 'weather' words with the missing letters.**

1 Yesterday was c _o_ _l_ _d_, but today it's really f_ _ _zin_ ! It's a bit w_ _ _ y, too.

2 It was nice and w_ _ _ yesterday. But today is even better: it's s_ _ ny, h_t and d_y!

3 It's a horrible day today. It's c_ _ _dy and cold. This morning it was r_ _ _y, so it's w_t here, too.

4 When it's f_ _ _ _ like today, it's hard to see where you're going!

4 **Complete the text with words from Exercise 3.**

I'm from Britain but I live in Brasilia, the capital of Brazil. The weather here is usually good – the temperature is normally between about 12° and 28°C, so it's never really [0]____*cold*____ . Sometimes in summer it's really [1]h_____ , but a lot of the time it's just nice and [2]w_____ , especially in the evenings.

There is one period in the year – from about May to July or August – when it rarely rains. So everything is very [3]d_____ . At other times of the year, the weather can be [4]r_____ and when it rains, it rains really hard!

Some days in the morning, when you wake up, the sky is grey and [5]c_____ , but then the clouds go away and the morning can be bright and [6]s_____ .

So, the weather here is quite nice, really – not like my home country, Britain, where it's often [7]f_____ in winter! I haven't seen ice here.

WordWise: Phrases with *with* → SB p.87

5 ★☆☆ **Complete the sentences with the phrases in the list.**

> busy with | good with | to do with
> with tomato sauce | with you
> ~~with 220 bedrooms~~

0 It's a big hotel *with 220 bedrooms* .

1 **A** Isn't Alice here?
   B No. I thought she came _____ .

2 It's delicious – pasta _____ and chicken.

3 She looks after my little brother. She's really _____ children.

4 Please don't ask me about it. It's got nothing _____ you.

5 I phoned him but he didn't answer. He was _____ his homework.

REFERENCE

THE WEATHER

cloudy   dry freezing humid sunny wet

cold foggy hot rainy warm windy

GEOGRAPHICAL FEATURES

beach   desert   forest   hill   island   jungle   lake   mountain   ocean   river

PHRASES WITH *WITH*

be with someone

be busy with something

be good with (animals / children ...)

something / someone with (big windows / chocolate sauce / long hair ...)

It's got nothing to do with (you / me / us ...)

VOCABULARY *EXTRA*

1 **Write the words under the photos.**

cave | ~~cliff~~ | countryside | grass | pond | trees

0 _____ *cliff* _____

1 _____

2 _____

3 _____

4 _____

5 _____

2 **Where can you find the things below where you live?**

0 grass _____ *the football field* _____

1 cave _____

2 cliffs _____

3 pond _____

4 countryside _____

5 trees _____

READING

1 Read the article and label each photo with the name of the place: *The Arctic* or *Antarctica*.

1 _____

POLE to POLE

2 _____

The Arctic and Antarctica are some of the wildest and most interesting places on Earth. Scientists study them because they can help us understand the history of our planet and the effects of climate change.

So, what do you know about the Arctic and Antarctica? Most people know that they are very cold and icy, but not many people know about the differences between them.

The Arctic is in the north and the Antarctic is in the south. There are around 4 million people who live in the Arctic, but no one lives in Antarctica all the time. There's more than just snow and ice to see in both places. There are beautiful wild landscapes and some very special animals. However, polar bears and penguins don't live in the same place – so forget what you see in cartoons! In the sea around both places you can see seals, whales and fish.

4 _____

And what about the weather? It's certainly freezing cold, but here's a surprise: a few parts of the Arctic and most of Antarctica get almost no rain or snow, so they are among the driest places on Earth. Antarctica is actually the world's largest desert!

More facts about these unusual places:

The Arctic	Antarctica
Climate **Average temperature** North Pole: 0°C – -40°C **Wind** Strong winds	**Climate** **Average temperature** South Pole: -28°C – -60°C **Wind** Windiest place on Earth
Landscape **Ice** (up to 5 m thick) + snow **Mountains** (highest: 3,694 m) Also grass, lakes, rivers – not many trees	**Landscape** **Ice** (up to 4.7 km thick) + snow **Mountains** (highest: 4,892 m) A few very small plants – no grass or trees
Animals Polar bears, seals, whales, fish, reindeer, foxes, wolves	**Animals** Penguins, seals, whales, fish
21 June **Summer:** 24 hrs light **21 December** **Winter:** 24 hrs dark	**21 June** **Winter:** 24 hrs dark **21 December** **Summer:** 24 hrs light

3 _____

2 Read the first part of the text and mark the sentences T (true) or F (false). Correct the false sentences.

1 Scientists think Antarctica is more interesting than the Arctic. ☐

2 More people live in the Arctic than in Antarctica. ☐

3 The same animals live in both places. ☐

4 There are penguins in the Arctic. ☐

5 Antarctica is the world's largest desert. ☐

3 Read the information in the table and complete the sentences with *the Arctic* or *Antarctica*.

0 ___*The Arctic*___ is warmer than ___*Antarctica*___ .

1 _____ is the coldest place on Earth.

2 _____ is windier than _____ .

3 The ice in _____ is thinner than in _____ .

4 _____ has got higher mountains than _____ .

5 Plants are rarer in _____ than in _____ .

6 There are more land animals in _____ than in _____ .

7 21 June is lighter in _____ than in _____ .

4 **CRITICAL THINKING** What is the purpose of this text? Choose the correct answer.

A To compare the Arctic and Antarctica.

B To talk about the animals that live in the North Pole.

C To explain why scientists are interested in the Arctic and Antarctica.

5 What do you think? Tick the sentences you agree with and explain why.

1 We must protect wild places on the planet. ☐
_____

2 We need to act quickly to stop climate change. ☐
_____

3 The Arctic and Antarctica are good places to live. ☐
_____

4 It's important to learn about animals in danger. ☐
_____

DEVELOPING ⟩ *Writing*

An email about a place

1 **INPUT** **Read Jake's email to Monika and answer the questions.**

1 Where is Monika going on holiday?

_____

2 Which two places does Jake recommend?

_____

Monika
Monika@thinkmail.com

Hey Monika,

So, you're going to South Korea? Lucky you! I went to South Korea two years ago with my family. It's a great place and I enjoyed it a lot. The food, the people, the places – so different from my country!

Anyway, I'm writing to give you some ideas. People usually arrive in Seoul and stay there for a few days. So when you're in Seoul, don't miss the Gyeongbokgung Palace! It's just fabulous. Here's a photo I took. You have to go there!

I know you like beaches and swimming so make sure you go to Jeju Island. It's in the south and you can swim, go diving and see lots of wonderful fish. It's very beautiful there.

Also, don't forget to listen to the music! K-pop's the best!

Sorry, I must go now – but just write if you want any more ideas!

Have a great holiday!

Jake

2 **ANALYSE** **Read Jake's email again. Underline the adjectives that he uses to give his opinion of things in South Korea.**

1 Are the adjectives positive or negative?

_____

2 Does Jake use any adjectives that are new for you? Look them up in a dictionary if you need to.

3 **Complete the phrases that Jake uses.**

0 _____*Don't miss*_____ Gyeongbokgung Palace.

1 You _____ go there!

2 _____ you go to Jeju Island.

3 _____ to listen to the music.

4 **What is Jake doing when he writes the sentences in Exercise 3?**

A Recommending / giving advice ☐

B Giving directions ☐

C Giving an opinion ☐

PRONUNCIATION
Vowel sounds: /ɪ/ and /aɪ/   Go to page 120.

✏ WRITING TIP: an informal email

- Organise the information into paragraphs.
- Use informal phrases. (*Lucky you! It's just fabulous! The food/music/weather is the best!*)
- Begin and end with a friendly phrase. (*Hi, Hey / Have fun, Write soon, See you soon, Have a great time/holiday!*)

5 **PLAN** **You want to tell an English-speaking friend about a place that you know and like. Make notes about:**

- why the place is special

_____

_____

- some adjectives you can use to describe it

_____

_____

- the best places to visit

_____

_____

- the most exciting things to do

_____

_____

6 **PRODUCE** **Write your email to your friend in 120–140 words. Use Jake's email to help you.**

🎧 LISTENING

1 🔊 9.04 **Listen to the conversations. Mark the sentences T (true) or F (false).**

Conversation 1

0 The girl wants to go to the beach. [F]

1 The girl doesn't know what a jigsaw puzzle is. ☐

2 The girl doesn't want to do a jigsaw puzzle. ☐

3 It's raining. ☐

Conversation 2

4 It's a cloudy day. ☐

5 The boy doesn't want to wear trousers. ☐

6 The boy likes the girl's T-shirt. ☐

7 The girl doesn't understand the words on her T-shirt. ☐

2 🔊 9.04 **Listen again. Complete the lines from the conversations.**

Conversation 1

Boy What a ⁰_____*horrible*_____ day today.

Girl Yes, it ¹_____ .

Boy I just thought, well, something different, ²_____ a jigsaw puzzle.

Girl What a ³_____ ! On a rainy day like today, it's a nice thing to do!

Conversation 2

Boy Wow, ⁴_____ fantastic day. It's so warm and ⁵_____ !

Girl So let's ⁶_____ somewhere.

Girl Hey, nice shorts. They ⁷_____ cool.

Boy Thanks. And I really like your T-shirt – what a ⁸_____ colour!

DIALOGUE

3 🔊 9.05 **Complete the conversation with the words in the list.**

> ~~can~~ | can't | idea | let's | maybe | perhaps

Boy What a horrible day. It's cold and snowing.

Girl I know. What ⁰_____*can*_____ we do?

Boy Well, we ¹_____ go outside.
So, ²_____ do something here.

Girl Well, ³_____ we can watch a film.

Boy Well, OK, yes. Or ⁴_____ we could play some video games.

Girl That's a good ⁵_____ .

4 **Write a conversation for this picture. Use some of the expressions in Exercises 2 and 3.**

Park?

Wow, new bike.

_____

_____

_____

_____

_____

_____

PHRASES FOR FLUENCY → SB p.90

5 🔊 9.06 **Put the conversation in order. Then listen and check.**

☐ **A** No problem. I'll call Jenny in a minute, she'll probably know.

☐ **A** Oh, yes, that's fixed it! Well done. Thank you!

[1] **A** Can you help me with my laptop? Something's wrong with it, and I don't know much about laptops.

☐ **A** Oh! So you can't help me, then?

☐ **B** Not really. I'm sorry.

☐ **B** Good idea. She's really good with these things. Oh – hang on! How about if you press this button here?

☐ **B** I don't know much either.

6 **Complete the phone conversation. Use the phrases in the list.**

> either | ~~in a minute~~
> no problem | not really | then

A Hi, John? Sorry, I'm a bit late. But I'll be at your place ⁰_____*in a minute*_____ .

B ¹_____ , Max. Is there a lot of traffic, ²_____ ?

A ³_____ . But I'm cycling and it's raining.

B Ugh. I hate cycling in the rain!

A I don't really like it ⁴_____ .
But I haven't got any money for the bus. Anyway, I shouldn't really be cycling and talking on the phone at the same time. Bye!

A2 Key for Schools

 READING AND WRITING

Part 4: 3-option multiple-choice cloze

1 For each question, choose the correct answer.

Alice Springs

Alice Springs is in Australia. The town is in the centre of the country. About 24,000 people live there, and it is the [1] … town in the area. It is 1500 km away from the cities of Adelaide and Darwin. The area [2]… the town is a desert. It is very dry with red [3] … and rocks. Outside Alice Springs, there are mountains, and Uluru is not [4] … away. Uluru is a large and famous red rock that looks like it changes colour at different times of the day. The weather in Alice Springs is very hot, and it doesn't rain very much. In summer, the temperatures can be [5] … , around 36°C, and the winters are [6] … at around 20°C.

1 A biggest	**B** bigger	**C** big
2 A around	**B** inside	**C** between
3 A sea	**B** island	**C** sand
4 A close	**B** far	**C** near
5 A high	**B** higher	**C** highest
6 A freezing	**B** warm	**C** foggy

EXAM GUIDE: READING AND WRITING PART 4

In A2 Key for Schools Reading and Writing Part 4, you have to choose one word to complete each gap. This exercise tests your understanding of words in context.

- First, read the text without worrying about the gaps. It's important to know what the text is about before you start the exercise.
- Some of the gaps test vocabulary, so you have to choose the word with the right meaning. Re-read the sentence before and after the gap to help you decide.
- Other gaps are about grammar, so re-read the sentence with the gap and try each of the options to see which sounds best.
- Always choose one of the words. Never leave a blank space.

2 Read the email about Niagara Falls. Choose the correct word (A, B or C) for each gap.

Here we are at Niagara Falls!

It's one of the [1] … amazing places in the world. There are three waterfalls here on the border between the US and Canada.
It's a fantastic place. However, Niagara Falls isn't [2] … highest waterfall in the world (that's the Angel Falls in Venezuela), but it is very big. When you are close to it, the noise from the water is so [3] … you can't hear other people talking!
It's one of the most [4] … places to visit in North America with over 30 million visitors a year. There are lots of ways to see the falls. The [5] … way to get close is by boat. Visitors can also get a great [6] … of the falls from an island in the Niagara River.

1 A more	**B** much	**C** most
2 A than	**B** the	**C** a
3 A loud	**B** big	**C** high
4 A dangerous	**B** popular	**C** exciting
5 A best	**B** first	**C** good
6 A visit	**B** view	**C** experience

10 OUT AND ABOUT

Grammar rap!
▶29

GRAMMAR

be going to for intentions

→ SB p.94

1 ⭐☆☆ **Complete the sentences with the verb *to be*. Use short forms.**

0 We ___'re___ going to see a show at the concert hall.

1 I _____ going to buy some sun cream at the chemist's.

2 They _____ going to the sports centre to play tennis.

3 We _____ going to have lunch at the shopping mall.

4 Taylor _____ going to catch the bus home.

2 ⭐⭐☆ **Complete the questions. Then match them with the answers.**

0 ___Are___ you going ___to watch___ the game? (watch) `e`

1 _____ they going _____ in a hotel? (stay) ☐

2 _____ we going _____ Gran this weekend? (visit) ☐

3 _____ Daniel going _____ a taxi? (take) ☐

4 _____ Jo going _____ the competition? (enter) ☐

5 _____ Andrés going _____ tonight? (cook) ☐

a No, they aren't. They're going camping.

b No, he's going to walk there.

c Yes, she is. She says she's feeling lucky.

d I hope so. He's really good at it.

e Yes, I am. I love football.

f Yes, we are. We're going to go on Sunday.

3 ⭐⭐☆ **Complete the answers with *going to* and the verbs in brackets.**

What **0**___are you going to do___ (do) when you leave school?

A 'I **1**_____ (study) Maths at Nottingham University. Two of my friends **2**_____ (go) there too, so we **3**_____ (find) a house to rent.'

B 'I'm not sure. My best friend **4**_____ (travel) around the world, and he wants me to go with him. I **5**_____ (not do) that – I haven't got enough money – but I **6**_____ (not go) to university either.'

4 ⭐⭐⭐ **Write five plans you have for this year. Use *going to*.**

I'm going to ... _____

_____

_____

_____

_____

Present continuous for arrangements

→ SB p.95

5 ⭐⭐☆ **Look at Claire's diary. Complete the sentences with the present continuous of the verbs.**

	MORNING	AFTERNOON	EVENING
MONDAY		tennis – Sue	kids – cinema
TUESDAY	breakfast with Tom		
WEDNESDAY			party at Nicole's
THURSDAY	meeting with Jen	dentist – 4 pm	
FRIDAY	golf		fly to Rome

0 Claire and Sue _____*are playing*_____ (play) tennis on Monday afternoon.

1 Claire _____ (fly) to Rome on Friday evening.

2 Claire _____ (go) to Nicole's party on Wednesday evening.

3 Claire _____ (go) to the dentist on Thursday afternoon.

4 Claire and Tom _____ (have) breakfast on Tuesday morning.

5 Claire _____ (play) golf on Friday morning.

6 Claire and her children _____ (go) to the cinema on Monday evening.

7 Claire and Jen _____ (have) a meeting on Thursday morning.

6 ★★★ Write the questions for the answers about Claire's week. Use the present continuous.

0 *Is Claire going to the dentist on Thursday?*

Yes, she is. Her appointment is at 4 pm.

1 _____

No, they're having breakfast.

2 _____

No, she's flying in the evening.

3 _____

Yes, but they don't know what film to see yet.

4 _____

That's right. They're playing in the afternoon.

7 ★★☆ Mark the sentences P (present) or F (future arrangement).

0 Henry's not at home. He's fishing with his dad. ☐ P

1 Sorry, I can't help you. I'm studying. ☐

2 Are you doing anything this evening? ☐

3 Look at the baby! She's trying to walk. ☐

4 Is Aunt Mary coming to stay next week? ☐

5 We're going to the skatepark this afternoon. ☐

6 I'm staying at my friend's house on Friday. ☐

8 ★★★ Write five arrangements you have for this weekend. Use the present continuous.

Adverbs

→ SB p.97

9 ★☆☆ Read the sentences. Write the names under the pictures.

Bella paints really well.
Molly paints quite badly.
Tom rides his bike dangerously.
Sam rides his bike carefully.

0 *Molly*   **2** _____

1 _____   **3** _____

10 ★★☆ Unscramble the words to make adjectives. Then write the adverbs.

		adjective	adverb
0	saye	*easy*	*easily*
1	wols	_____	_____
2	kiquc	_____	_____
3	souranged	_____	_____
4	revosun	_____	_____
5	teiqu	_____	_____
6	dab	_____	_____
7	larefuc	_____	_____
8	dogo	_____	_____

11 ★★★ Circle the correct words.

0 Jackson played very *good / well* and won the match *easy / easily*.

1 It was an *easy / easily* test and I finished it really *quick / quickly*.

2 My dad isn't a very *careful / carefully* driver and sometimes he drives quite *dangerous / dangerously*.

3 Please be *quiet / quietly* in the library – you can talk, but not too *loud / loudly*.

4 I didn't do *good / well* in the test – I had a really *bad / badly* day.

5 He's quite a *nervous / nervously* person and he talks really *quiet / quietly*.

GET IT RIGHT!

Adverbs

Adverbs usually come immediately after the object of the sentence or after the verb (if there is no object). They never come between the verb and the object.

✓ He drives his car dangerously.

✗ He ~~drives dangerously~~ his car.

Rewrite the sentences. Change the adjective in brackets into an adverb and put it in the correct place.

0 He can run fast, but he can't swim. (good)

He can run fast, but he can't swim well.

1 You should drive when it's raining. (slow)

_____

2 Hold the baby. (careful)

_____

3 We were walking because we were late for school. (fast)

_____

4 They did the homework because they worked together. (easy)

_____

VOCABULARY
Places in town

→ SB p.94

1 ★☆☆ Look at the pictures and complete the words for places.

0 c_o_nc_e_rt h_a_ll

4 p__l__ce st__t__ __n

1 b__s st__t __ __n

5 p __ st __ff__ c__

2 f__ __ tb__ll st__d__ __ m

6 sp__rts c__ntr__

3 c__r p__r k

7 s__op __in__ m__ll

2 ★★☆ Complete the text with words from Exercise 1.

Our town is great. It's got everything I need. There's a really good sports ⁰_____ centre _____ . You can do lots of different sports. There's a big ¹_____ hall as well, and I often go to see my favourite bands there. Most Saturdays, I go to the football ²_____ to see our football team play. There's a really big shopping ³_____ with lots of shops in it. And if you ever get bored, you can go to the bus ⁴_____ to catch a bus and visit another town.

3 ★★★ Where are these people? Choose from the places in Exercise 1.

0 'What time does the swimming pool close?' _____ sports centre _____

1 'I want to send this letter to Australia.' _____

2 'I think Manchester United are going to win today.' _____

3 'What time is the next bus to Liverpool?' _____

4 'I want to buy some new shoes.' _____

5 'The band starts playing at 8 pm.' _____

6 'It costs £2 for every hour we stay.' _____

7 'There's a problem at the bank. Come quickly.' _____

Things in town: compound nouns

→ SB p.97

4 ★☆☆ Write compound nouns using a word from each list.

| bill | ~~cycle~~ | graffiti | litter | speed | youth | zebra |

| bin | board | camera | club | crossing | ~~lane~~ | wall |

0 _____ cycle lane _____ **4** _____

1 _____ **5** _____

2 _____ **6** _____

3 _____

5 ★★☆ Match the nouns from Exercise 4 with the definitions.

0 It checks how fast cars are going. _____ speed camera _____

1 You can ride your bike safely here. _____

2 It advertises things on the side of the road. _____

3 Cross the road safely here. _____

4 A great place for young artists to paint. _____

5 A place to meet friends and have fun. _____

6 Throw your rubbish in this. _____

6 ★★☆ Which of these sentences are true about your town? Correct the ones that are false.

1 Cars always stop at zebra crossings.

2 There are lots of things for young people to do. There are graffiti walls and really good youth clubs.

3 Speed cameras make the roads safer.

4 You can get everywhere on your bike using cycle lanes.

5 People always use the litter bins to throw away rubbish.

6 There are lots of billboards.

7 The high street is full of shoppers at the weekend.

REFERENCE

post office

police station

sports centre

shopping mall

car park

football stadium

concert hall

bus station

THINGS IN A TOWN

zebra crossing

youth club

speed camera

graffiti wall

cycle lane

litter bin

billboard

high street

VOCABULARY *EXTRA*

1 Match the words to make compound nouns.

0	play	**a**	way	**0**	*playground*	
1	air	**b**	station	**1**	_____	
2	motor	**c**	port	**2**	_____	
3	city	**d**	ground	**3**	_____	
4	under	**e**	centre	**4**	_____	
5	railway	**f**	ground	**5**	_____	

2 Write the name of a place in your country for each of these things.

1 A football stadium: _____

2 A city with an underground: _____

3 A busy motorway: _____

4 The nearest playground to your school: _____

5 An interesting city centre: _____

6 The biggest airport: _____

UNUSUAL TOWNS

 Monowi, US

The town of Monowi in Nebraska is perhaps one of the most unusual places in the US – and all because of Elsie Eiler. That's because Elsie is the only person who lives there. Monowi was never a big town. In the 1930s, the population was 150, but over the years people slowly started leaving. In 2000, there were only two people left: Elsie and her husband, Rudy. When Rudy died, Elsie became the only citizen.

 Thames Town, China

Shanghai is one of China's biggest cities. But just outside of Shanghai is a very different place called Thames Town. It cost £500 million to build and it is part of their 'One City, Nine Towns' project. When you walk down the streets there, you can easily forget you are in China!

That's because Thames Town is a copy of an English town. The streets and the buildings all look English. It has red phone boxes, London street signs, fish and chip shops and English pubs. There are also statues of Harry Potter and James Bond. Elsewhere in China, you can find the Eiffel Tower, an Austrian village and even Stonehenge.

 Sheffield, Australia

In the 1980s, the citizens of Sheffield on the Australian island of Tasmania decided they wanted more tourists to visit their town. They had an idea to turn their streets into an outdoor art gallery. They asked artists to paint huge paintings on the walls around town. Children from the local school helped, too – they painted little murals on the rubbish bins. There are now more than 100 murals, which include landscapes and scenes from history. The plan worked, and these days about 220,000 people visit Sheffield every year.

 Roswell, US

Some people believe that in 1947 an alien spacecraft crashed near the town of Roswell in New Mexico. They believe that the American military seized this UFO and took it to a secret place outside of the town. It's a strange idea, but people love mysteries like this. These days Roswell sees many tourists who are interested in life on other planets. There are lots of shops that sell souvenirs and there is one fast food restaurant with a UFO theme. There is also a museum about aliens.

1 _____

2 _____

READING

1 **Read the article. Which towns can you see in the pictures? Write their names.**

2 **Read the article again. Write the names of the towns after the sentences.**

0	People think there were aliens here.	*Roswell*
1	They wanted more people to visit here.	_____
2	It has a population of one.	_____
3	It's near to a really big city.	_____
4	People didn't want to live here.	_____
5	It's like being in another country.	_____
6	It's a mysterious place.	_____
7	It's a great place if you like art.	_____

3 **CRITICAL THINKING** **Fact or opinion? Mark the sentences F (fact) or O (opinion).**

1 The town of Monowi in Nebraska must be one of the most unusual places in the US. ☐

2 When Rudy died, Elsie became the only citizen. ☐

3 Thames Town cost £500 million to build. ☐

4 You can easily forget you are in China! ☐

5 Children from the local school helped, too. ☐

6 It's a strange idea, but people love mysteries like this. ☐

DEVELOPING Writing

An informal email

Jess
jessjones@thinkmail.com

Hi Jess,

Thanks for your message. So sorry to hear about your accident – I'm really glad you're feeling better now.

I've got some big news: we're moving house next month! We're going to live in Bristol and we're leaving on 25 July. The new house is quite big and I'm finally going to have my own bedroom! I can't wait! The rooms look a bit sad at the moment, but we're going to paint the walls and get some new furniture.

So I'm starting in a new school in September! I'm a bit nervous about that. But it's exciting, too. I really love Bristol – it's got great shops and cinemas, and there's a cool skatepark near our house.

You must come to visit SOON. I miss you loads! We're going to have a party on the second Sunday in August! Do you want to come? Let me know.

Send my love to your mum.

Love,

Lauren

1 **INPUT** **Read Lauren's email and answer the questions.**

0 Why is Lauren writing to Jess?
To tell her she is moving to Bristol.

1 When are her family leaving their old home?
_____

2 Why is the new house especially good for Lauren?
_____

3 What are they going to do to make the house look better?
_____

4 How does Lauren feel about going to a new school?
_____

5 What is going to happen in August?
_____

2 **ANALYSE** **Read the email again and find expressions that mean the same as 1–4.**

1 I'm very sad about (your bad news)
_____

2 I'm excited
_____

3 I really want you to (do something)
_____

4 Say hello to (someone) from me
_____

 WRITING TIP: an informal email

- We write informal emails to friends, family and people we know well.
- Informal emails should be friendly and show personal interest in the other person.
- Use informal language, for example, short forms, direct questions, exclamation marks (!) and dashes (–).
- Organise the email into paragraphs:
  - First, greet your friend and comment on any news from him/her.
  - Then give your news.
  - Write the facts but also describe how you feel and give your opinions.

3 **PLAN** **Choose ONE of these situations. Complete the plan with short notes for the email you are going to write.**

- Your friend from the country is coming to your town for the first time and wants to know what it's like. Write and tell them.
- You're going on a school trip to a big city. Write to a friend to give them the news and tell them a bit about the city you're going to visit.
- It's the first day of your holiday. Write to your friend and tell them about the town where you are staying and your plans for the holiday.

Paragraph 1	
Paragraph 2	
Paragraph 3	

4 **PRODUCE** **Write your email to a friend in about 120–150 words.**

🎧 LISTENING

1 🔊 **10.01** Listen to the conversations and tick (✓) the correct box in the table.

	Invitation accepted	Invitation not accepted
Conversation 1		
Conversation 2		
Conversation 3		

2 🔊 **10.01** Listen again and complete the sentences.

Conversation 1

Hannah invites Daniel to the ⁰ _sports centre_ .

He can't go because he's got ¹_____ .

Daniel says they can go ²_____ .

Conversation 2

Isabelle invites Marcus to a ³_____ on ⁴_____ .

The ticket costs ⁵_____ .

They are going to meet outside the ⁶_____ at 8.

Conversation 3

Chloe says she hasn't got any ⁷_____ for the ⁸_____ .

Luke and his friends are thinking of going to the ⁹_____ .

Chloe is interested in going to the ¹⁰_____ on Ice.

DIALOGUE

3 🔊 **10.02** Complete the two conversations with the sentences A–H. Then listen and check.

A How about next week?

B We're meeting outside the concert hall at 8.

C That would be great!

D I've got music practice this afternoon.

E See you then.

F Let's see.

G No! Sorry.

H How much is the ticket?

Conversation 1

Hannah Hi, Daniel. Do you want to go to the sports centre after school today?

Daniel Hannah, hi! No, sorry, I can't. ⁰_D_

Hannah What about tomorrow?

Daniel Yes, I think I can. ¹__ I'm meeting Martin.

Hannah Are you free any day this week?

Daniel No, I'm really busy. ²__

Hannah OK. ³__

Conversation 2

Isabelle Marcus, would you like to come to the Jax concert with us on Wednesday?

Marcus Wow! Yes, please. ⁴__ ! Thanks, Isabelle!

Isabelle We've got an extra ticket because Callum can't come.

Marcus Cool! ⁵__

Isabelle It's only £25 because it's a student ticket. ⁶__ Is that OK?

Marcus Great. ⁷__ .

4 Write two short conversations for these situations.

Conversation 1

Boy invites girl to cinema.

She says yes.

They agree on a time.

Conversation 2

Girl invites boy to party.

He asks what day and where.

He can't make it and says why.

Train to TH!NK

Problem solving

5 The town council has money to build one new building. Look at the suggestions and match them with the advantages and disadvantages.

> bad for shops on high street | creates lots of jobs
> ~~good to get bands into town~~ | more cars in town
> noisy at night | stops people parking on street

Suggestions	Advantage	Disadvantage
1 concert hall	good to get bands into town	
2 shopping mall		
3 car park		

6 Think of an advantage and a disadvantage for these three suggestions.

Suggestions	Advantage	Disadvantage
1 football stadium		
2 bus station		
3 sports centre		

7 Complete the statement. Use your own ideas.

I think the _____ is the best idea

because _____

and _____ .

> **PRONUNCIATION**
> Voiced /ð/ and unvoiced /θ/ consonants
> Go to page 121. 🎧

A2 Key for Schools

📖 READING AND WRITING
Part 5: open cloze

1 For each question, write the correct answer. Write ONE word for each gap.

> ✉ New message   — ✎ ✕
>
> ### A WEEKEND VISIT
>
> I ⁰____*am*____ really excited! Next weekend, we are going to stay with my uncle and ¹_____ family. They live ²_____ a really nice flat near the city centre. My uncle is planning a busy weekend ³_____ us. We are going to walk around ⁴_____ city on Saturday morning. In the afternoon, my cousin Milly and I want to visit a museum ⁵_____ the rest of the family go on a boat on the river. On Sunday, we're all going to the stadium to ⁶_____ a rugby match. It's going to be the best weekend ever!

EXAM GUIDE: READING AND WRITING PART 5

In A2 Key for Schools Reading and Writing Part 5, you have to complete a short email or message. There is an example at the beginning and then you have to write ONE word in each of the six gaps.

- This exercise focuses on grammar, so you need to think about verbs, questions, negatives, prepositions, articles and pronouns.
- Always look at the words immediately <u>before</u> and <u>after</u> the gaps because they can help you find the right word.
- Try a word in the gap, then read the sentence again to see if it sounds right.

Contracted verb forms are not tested in this part of the exam.

2 For each question, write the correct answer. Write ONE word for each gap.

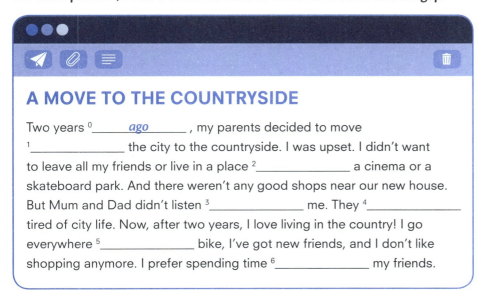

> ### A MOVE TO THE COUNTRYSIDE
>
> Two years ⁰____*ago*____ , my parents decided to move ¹_____ the city to the countryside. I was upset. I didn't want to leave all my friends or live in a place ²_____ a cinema or a skateboard park. And there weren't any good shops near our new house. But Mum and Dad didn't listen ³_____ me. They ⁴_____ tired of city life. Now, after two years, I love living in the country! I go everywhere ⁵_____ bike, I've got new friends, and I don't like shopping anymore. I prefer spending time ⁶_____ my friends.

CONSOLIDATION

🎧 LISTENING

1 🔊 10.04 **Listen to the conversations. Choose the correct answer A, B or C. Then listen and check.**

1 What kind of holiday is Emma going to suggest to her parents?

A hotel   B houseboat   C camping

2 Who's got the best idea about what they can do?

A Mike   B Dad   C Mum

3 When are Emma and her family going on holiday?

A 4 July   B 18 July   C 8 August

2 🔊 10.04 **Listen again and answer the questions.**

0 Why don't Mike and Emma want to go to the same hotel as last year?

They think it would be boring.

1 What does Emma think of the idea of a camping holiday?

_____

2 What does Dad think about Emma's suggestion of a holiday on a houseboat?

_____

3 What is Mum going to suggest to the grandparents?

_____

4 Mum makes a joke. What does she say?

_____

5 How soon are Emma and her family going on their holiday?

_____

🔤 VOCABULARY

3 Circle **the correct words.**

Before you go on a holiday, you need to think carefully about where you want to go. If you decide to go to a place in the ⁰(mountains) / beach, for example, you have to know that the weather can be ¹*freezing / hot* (even in summer), and it can also be quite ²*windy / warm*. Everybody knows that deserts are ³*dry / wet*, but people sometimes forget that a ⁴*beach / forest* holiday means you are close to a lot of water, so the air can be quite ⁵*dry / humid*. This can mean you feel ⁶*hotter / colder* and not everybody likes that. Here are my family's plans for our next holiday. My parents love sailing, so we're going to ⁷*spend / spending* two weeks camping near a ⁸*hill / lake*. Then, on 1 September, we are ⁹*leaving / leave* for a weekend in the mountains.

4 **Complete the sentences. Use the words in the list.**

> billboard | ~~concert hall~~ | cycle lane | litter bin
> post office | speed camera | zebra crossing

0 I can't believe we can't get tickets for the show. There's room for 2,000 people in the _concert hall_ .

1 I need some stamps. Can you go to the _____ for me?

2 Careful – don't drive so fast! There's a _____ ahead, so keep to 50 km/h, OK?

3 I want to throw this paper away. Is there a _____ around here?

4 Did you see that driver?! There was someone on the _____ and he didn't stop!

5 A road is much safer for cycling if there's a _____ .

6 There was an advertisement for his new album on the _____ .

 GRAMMAR

5 Circle **the correct words.**

Laurence When are you going on holiday?

Oscar Next weekend. And we're all looking forward to it. It's going to be the ⁰*better* / (best) holiday ever!

Laurence Are you going to the same place as last year?

Oscar Yes, we are. We had a brilliant time last year.

Laurence Is it ¹*hotter / hottest* than here?

Oscar Not really. It's ²*more cold / colder* than here, and there's usually ³*more / most* wind. So the temperature is normally a few degrees lower ⁴*more / than* here.

Laurence I think it's the ⁵*more / most* beautiful beach on the west coast.

Oscar Do you think so? Well, it's ⁶*more / most* attractive than other places, but we can't swim in the ocean.

Laurence Can't you?

Oscar No, the water is just too cold. And I don't think it's ⁷*safe / safely*.

Laurence Oh, really. Are there any ⁸*dangerous / dangerously* fish?

Oscar I don't think there are. But the waves are really high because of the wind. You have to be able to swim really ⁹*good / well* to go in the sea. But then you get out ¹⁰*quick / quickly* because it's freezing!

DIALOGUE

6 🔊 **10.05** **Complete the conversation. Use the phrases in the list.**

> are going to | busy with | can't
> can't go | going to come | ~~going to go~~
> I'd | like | like to | no problem

Eva Jack, I'm ⁰_____*going to go*_____ to the concert on Saturday. Would you ¹_____ to come along? My friend Nick ²_____ , so I've got a ticket if you want it.

Jack Saturday? I'm sorry, I can't. I'm ³_____ a project.

Eva I see. Well, maybe another time.

Jack Yeah, thanks for asking. Oh, would you and Nick ⁴_____ come over to our place next Sunday, maybe? We can sit in the garden and enjoy the beautiful weather. George and Camilla ⁵_____ come, too.

Eva ⁶_____ love to. That would be great. Let me talk to Nick. I know he's going to visit some relatives on Saturday, but I think he's ⁷_____ back on Sunday morning. So it should be fine. Can I tell you this evening?

Jack ⁸_____ . Talk to Nick first and call me any time.

Later, on the phone …

Jack Hello?

Eva Oh, hi, Jack. It's about next Sunday. I'm really sorry. Nick ⁹_____ make it on Sunday. He's coming back late in the evening, so I'm going to come alone.

Jack OK.

📖 READING

7 **Read the magazine article about Peru. For questions 1–3, choose the correct ending (A or B) for each sentence.**

0 Peru is very popular for holidays …
  (A) because there are lots of beautiful places to visit.
  B because the weather is always sunny.

1 A holiday on the coast in summer is good if you …
  A like hot, dry weather.
  B don't mind a lot of foggy and rainy days.

2 In the Andes, in winter it's usually …
  A foggy but not very cold.
  B dry, and it can be very, very cold.

3 In the east, there are no mountains and …
  A the weather doesn't change much.
  B there are extreme differences between seasons.

SO MANY KINDS OF WEATHER!

Peru isn't just a beautiful country. Tourists love it because of its attractive jungles, its stunning beaches and the fantastic Peruvian food. And many people come to see Machu Picchu, a very interesting Inca site that's more than 500 years old. But Peru is also famous for its many different climates. If you travel from one place to another, you can have very different weather on the same day! The weather on the coast is usually dry and warm, often hot. In the summer, it's hardly ever rainy there. In winter, the coast is often foggy, and the fog even has its own name, *garúa*. In the areas near the ocean, the so-called 'rainy season' starts around late May and comes to an end in October.

In the mountains, the famous Andes, it's often cool, and sometimes cold. The summers there are usually rainy, but the winters are very dry, and can be freezing. In the east, where there are no mountains, the weather is usually hot and humid all year round.

✏️ WRITING

8 **Write a paragraph about the weather in your country (about 80–100 words). Think about these questions.**

- What's the weather like in your area? What's the weather like in different parts of the country?

- When are the best times of the year for tourists to visit your country?

11 FUTURE BODIES

Grammar rap!

GRAMMAR

will / won't for future predictions

→ SB p.104

1 ★★☆ **Put the words in order to make sentences.**

0 'll / home / by / I / 7.30 / be
I'll be home by 7.30.

1 Sunday / home / and / we / stay / at / relax / On / 'll
_____

2 homework / your / finish / Will / soon / you
_____

3 you / I / to / know / where / find / Will
_____

4 come / the / party / to / won't / Sebastian
_____

2 ★★☆ **Complete the sentences. Use *will* and the verb in brackets. Then match sentences 1–5 with sentences a–f.**

0 Don't worry. I'm sure you ___*won't have*___ problems with the test. (not have) [e]

1 This year at school _____ cool. (be) ☐

2 I'm not sure a picnic is such a great idea. ☐

3 Kate's not sure if she _____ to the cinema tonight. (go) ☐

4 Brett and Mason _____ back from their trip soon. (be) ☐

5 Don't try to repair your bike without me. ☐

a Our teachers _____ probably _____ us to a youth camp in the last week before the holidays. (take)

b Perhaps she _____ at home and work on her project. (stay)

c It _____ probably _____ raining later today. (start)

d I'm sure they _____ lots of stories to tell. (have)

e You always study hard.

f Let's do it together. That _____ much more fun. (be)

3 ★★☆ **Complete the questions. Use *will* and the verbs in the list.**

get married | go | have (x 2) | ~~learn~~ | live

0 When ___*will*___ you ___*learn*___ to drive?

1 _____ you ever _____ in another country?

2 _____ you ever _____ a sports car?

3 How many children _____ you _____ ?

4 Do you think you _____ ?

5 _____ you _____ to university after school?

4 ★★★ **Complete the answers. Use *will* and the verbs in the list. Then match them with the questions in Exercise 3.**

do | drive | ~~have~~ | live | not get | take

0 I ___*'ll have*___ lots. I love children. [3]

1 Yes, I think I _____ that but I'm not sure what to study yet. ☐

2 Yes, I think so. But actually, I'm sure I _____ married before I'm 30. ☐

3 I think I _____ my driving test before I go to university. ☐

4 A sports car? No. I don't think I _____ ever even _____ a car. ☐

5 I think I _____ in Japan for a year before I go to university. ☐

5 ★★★ **Answer the questions in Exercise 3 so they are true for you.**

_____
_____
_____
_____
_____
_____

PRONUNCIATION
The /h/ consonant sound Go to page 121. 🎧

First conditional

→ SB p.106

6 ★★☆ **Match each picture with two sentences.**

0 I won't have a lot of money left if I order an ice cream. `b`

1 If his alarm clock doesn't ring, he won't wake up. ☐

2 The neighbours will get angry if he doesn't stop. ☐

3 If I don't have a snack now, I'll be hungry later. ☐

4 He'll be late for school if he doesn't get up soon. ☐

5 If he doesn't practise, he'll never play in a band. ☐

7 ★★☆ **For each sentence, choose the most likely ending, A or B.**

0 He won't pass the test
 Ⓐ if he doesn't study hard.
 B if he studies hard.

1 I'm sure all of your friends will come to your party
 A if you don't invite them.
 B if you invite them.

2 It's raining. If you don't put on your hat,
 A you'll get wet.
 B you won't get wet.

3 She'll book a trip to Rome
 A if it isn't too expensive.
 B if it's too expensive.

4 If we don't play better,
 A we'll win the match.
 B we'll lose the match.

5 If they find another of those T-shirts,
 A they won't get one for you.
 B they'll get one for you.

8 ★★★ **Complete the first conditional sentences with the correct form of the verbs.**

0 If you _don't listen_ (not listen), your teacher _won't tell_ (not tell) you what to do again.

1 If we _____ (not feed) the cat, she _____ (be) very hungry.

2 The police _____ (stop) him if he _____ (not slow down).

3 If we _____ (not use) a satnav, we _____ (not find) the way home.

4 Nobody _____ (talk) to them if they _____ (not be) friendly.

5 If Susie _____ (not help) me, I _____ (be) in trouble.

9 ★★★ **Complete the sentences with your predictions.**

50 years from now …

1 If all cars are driverless, _____ .

2 If time travel becomes possible, _____ .

3 If there are 10 billion people on Earth, _____ .

4 If computers can speak all languages, _____ .

5 If people can fly to Mars in 24 hours, _____ .

Time clauses with *when / as soon as*

→ SB p.107

10 ★★☆ Circle the correct words.

0 When we (arrive)/ *'ll arrive*, we *send* /('ll send) you a text message.

1 He *look* / *'ll look* for the keys as soon as he *'s* / *'ll be* home.

2 We *watch* / *'ll watch* the film as soon as the electricity *comes* / *will come* back on.

3 As soon as I *get* / *'ll get* the money, I *pay* / *'ll pay* you back.

4 I *take* / *'ll take* you to the new club when you *come* / *'ll come* and see us.

5 Dad *returns* / *will return* from the US as soon as his job there *is* / *will be* finished.

GET IT RIGHT!

First conditional

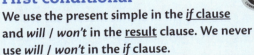

We use the present simple in the *if clause* and *will / won't* in the result clause. We never use *will / won't* in the *if* clause.

✓ If I **see** Rory, **I'll tell** him the news.

✗ If I ~~will see~~ Rory, I'll tell him the news.

Find four incorrect uses of *will*. Correct them.

I don't know what to do! I feel ill, but if I won't go to school tomorrow, I'll miss the test. If I'll miss the test, I'll have to do it in the holidays. I won't be able to go to London if I will have to do the test in the holidays. But if I will go to school tomorrow and do the test when I'm ill, I'm sure I won't get a good mark. What a difficult decision!

Ⓐ VOCABULARY
Parts of the body
→ SB p.104

1 ★☆☆ Unscramble the words to make parts of the body.

> alenk | asmotch | bolwe
> elusmc | cnek | ilp | tatroh

0 ___ankle___   4 _____
1 _____   5 _____
2 _____   6 _____
3 _____

2 ★★☆ Complete the sentences with words for parts of the body.

0 When he tried to put his shoe on his f_oot_ , he found that his a_nkle_ hurt.

1 This backpack is so heavy that all the m_____s in my n_____ and my s_____ s are hurting.

2 I've got a lot of pain all up my left arm. It hurts from the ends of my f_____ s, through my h_____ , and up to my e_____ .

3 I walked straight into a window. My whole face really hurts; my l_____ , my m_____ , my e_____s and my e_____s – they all hurt!

4 I ate too much. I've got s_____ ache.

3 ★★☆ Write verbs or phrases for actions that match the parts of the body. How many can you find?

foot – _run, walk,_____
mouth – _eat_____
ear – _listen to music,_____
arm – _____
eye – _____
fingers – _____
tongue – _____

when and *if*
→ SB p.107

4 ★☆☆ Circle the correct words.

0 Mum doesn't know when she'll be back. She'll phone us (if) / when she has to work late.

1 I can't do that now. I'll try to do it tomorrow if / when I've got time.

2 I'm not sure where my tablet is right now. I'll give it to you if / when I find it.

3 It's still dark outside. We'll start in an hour, if / when it's light.

4 It's Jane's birthday on Sunday. She'll be sad if / when you don't give her a present.

5 I'm checking my messages now. I'll be with you in a minute if / when I finish.

WordWise: Expressions with *do*
→ SB p.105

5 ★☆☆ Match the sentences with the pictures.

0 Let's go in there. They do great food. | c |

1 I'm happy to do the cooking, but it seems we need to go shopping first. | |

2 I think we need to do some cleaning here. | |

3 This has the latest technology. It does 30 kilometres to the litre. | |

4 And Dad thinks I'm doing my homework. Ha ha ha! | |

5 He isn't very well at the moment. I don't think he can play in the match today. | |

6 ★★☆ Complete the questions with the words in the list.

> cooking | exercise | homework | ice cream | well

0 A How often do you do _exercise_ in a week?
  B I go running on Mondays and Wednesdays, and go to the gym on Fridays.

1 A Did you do _____ in your last English test?
  B Yes, I got top marks.

2 A Who does the _____ in your family?
  B My mum. Her food is really good.

3 A Who does the best _____ in your town?
  B There's a new café on my street. It's wonderful.

4 A When do you usually do your _____ ?
  B Straight after school, when I can still remember everything.

7 ★★★ Answer the questions in Exercise 6 so they are true for you.

REFERENCE

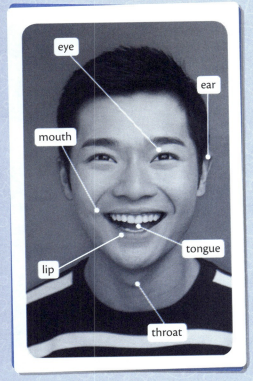

eye
ear
mouth
tongue
lip
throat

PARTS OF THE BODY

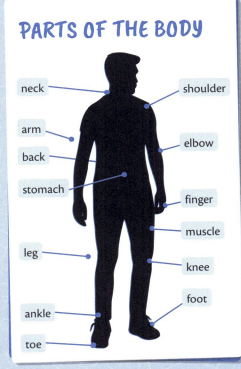

neck
arm
back
stomach
leg
ankle
toe
shoulder
elbow
finger
muscle
knee
foot

ACHES

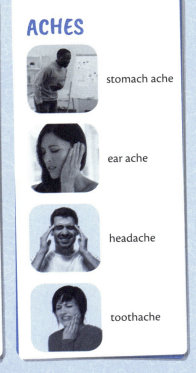

stomach ache

ear ache

headache

toothache

WHEN / IF

When we arrive, John will cook the dinner. (It is certain we will arrive.)

If we arrive before 10, John will cook the dinner. (It isn't certain we will arrive before 10.)

EXPRESSIONS WITH *DO*

do exercise

do the cleaning

do the cooking

do homework

do OK

do well

do (food / drink, in a café, restaurant, etc.)

do (12 kilometres to the litre)

VOCABULARY *EXTRA*

1   Unscramble the letters and write the words under the pictures.

eckhe | eehtt | dahe | irha | kins | reath

0   *cheek*   1 _____   2 _____   3 _____   4 _____   5 _____

2   Complete the sentences with the words in Exercise 1. Make them plural if you need to.

0   You should brush your ____*teeth*____ after every meal.

1   Penny has got lovely long brown _____ .

2   I was scared and my _____ was beating very fast.

3   My _____ is really dry. I need some cream.

4   Is it cold outside? Your nose and _____ are red!

5   Matt's very tall. The top of my _____ only reaches his shoulder!

FROM SCIENCE FICTION TO SCIENCE FACT

Technology is moving fast and changing our lives. We asked YOU, our readers, to tell us about inventions that you think will change our world and our health in the future!

1 _____

Hospitals already have some amazing machines, but soon they'll have robot nurses, too! Just like Baymax in *Big Hero 6*! I don't think people will wake up and find a robot standing next to their bed any time soon, but I read that scientists in Japan are creating robots to do some of the jobs nurses do. Robots will be useful for lifting and moving patients. This sounds great because if robots do the heavy work, nurses will have more time to look after individual patients.

Anton

2 _____

If you cut your leg or finger, it usually gets better quickly. But lots of people have very bad injuries that don't heal easily. The other day, I watched a video about a new gel to help these people. It seems to have incredible healing effects and I'm sure doctors will use it in the future. It made me think of a *Star Wars* film, when Luke Skywalker floated in a bath of healing gel to repair his body. Maybe that's where scientists got this idea!

Lachlan

3 _____

Yesterday, I read a great article about mind control. Scientists are now making a wheelchair you can control with your mind. When you think about where you want to go, the chair moves in the right direction. It means that users will be more independent. At the moment, the wheelchair can follow simple instructions like: *stop* or *go right*. It also has technology to stop it from hitting walls and furniture. Scientists are still working on it, so when it's ready, it will probably be able to do more.

Phoebe

READING

1 Read the blog. Match the headings with the paragraphs.

A Just think and move

B Computers that care for you

C A magical medicine

2 Match the comments with the paragraphs.

A I can't move my arms and legs. This will change my life. I hope I'll have one soon. ☐

B Great idea. It will help people get better more quickly. ☐

C I don't like this idea. When I'm really ill I want real people to help me! Old people and children won't like these, I'm sure. ☐

3 CRITICAL THINKING Complete the table with your ideas.

Invention	Who will this help?	Disadvantages
Robot nurses		
Healing gel		
Mind-controlled wheelchair		

DEVELOPING *Writing*

Taking phone messages

1 `INPUT` `🔊 11.02` **Listen to the conversation. Why can't Dylan take the call? Choose the correct answer.**

A He's out at the bank.

B He's out shopping.

C He's in a meeting.

2 `🔊 11.02` **Listen again. Then read Rachel's message for Dylan. Which two pieces of information in the message are wrong?**

1 _____

2 _____

> Dylan
> Gavin called from the fruit and vegetable company. He says he had a problem with his van and he's going to be late. He'll arrive at 5 pm. He doesn't have any tomatoes, but he asked if you want anything else instead. You can call him on his mobile.
> I'm going home now, but I'll see you next Saturday.
> Rachel

3 `ANALYSE` **Later, Rachel wrote this message to her mum. Compare it with her first message. Complete the sentences with the correct name, Dylan or Mum.**

> Mum
> Back from café. Julia phoned. Said yoga class is at 6 tomorrow. Asked if you need lift — can pick you up at 5.30. Will ring again later.
> Going to Fran's now. Back about 7 — see you then.
> Love,
> Rach

1 The message to _____ is informal.

2 The message to _____ is quite formal.

3 In the message to _____ Rachel wrote in full sentences.

4 In the message to _____ she left out some words.

4 **Rewrite Rachel's message to her mum in full sentences. Use the missing words in the list. You can use some words more than once.**

> a | at | I | I'll | I'll be | I'm | she | the

I'm back from the café.

WRITING TIP: taking a phone message

Listen carefully and make notes about the most important details:

- Who phoned?
- Who is the message for?
- What is the key information?

After the phone call, write out the message. If it's for someone you know well, you can leave out some words – but only if the message is still clear:

- articles (*the, a, an*)
- personal pronouns (*I, we, he, she*)
- possessive adjectives (*my, his, their*)
- verb *to be* (*am, is, are*)

5 **Make this message more informal. Cross out the words that can be left out.**

> Noah
> Thomas called. He wants to ask you about the French homework. He's finding it hard to understand. Also he's going to see the new film at the cinema tonight. Are you interested? Can you please contact him as soon as possible? His new phone number is 0679 645036.
> Robbie

6 `🔊 11.03` `PLAN` **Listen to the conversations and make notes.**

> Call from: _____
> Message for: _____
> Information: _____
> _____
> _____
> _____
>
> Call from: _____
> Message for: _____
> Information: _____
> _____
> _____
> _____

7 `PRODUCE` **Write your two phone messages.**

- Decide whether the message is formal or informal.
- Include all the important information.
- When your messages are finished, read them again. Ask yourself, 'Will the message be clear to the person who reads it?'

LISTENING

1 🔊 **11.04** **Listen to the conversations. Choose the correct answer A, B or C.**

Conversation 1

1 How does Lee feel about the Biology project?
- **A** fed up
- **B** excited
- **C** bored

Conversation 2

2 How does Ryan see the future of food?
- **A** We'll eat pills.
- **B** We won't eat cakes.
- **C** We'll still eat the same food.

Conversation 3

3 What does Milly think Sofia should do to get fit?
- **A** go to the gym
- **B** go dancing
- **C** walk on the beach

2 🔊 **11.04** **Listen again and mark the sentences T (true) or F (false).**

Conversation 1

1 Lee won't enjoy the project. ☐

2 Laura and Lee will have to work hard. ☐

Conversation 2

3 Ryan enjoys making cakes. ☐

4 Ava thinks that perhaps people will eat space food. ☐

Conversation 3

5 Milly is on her way to the park. ☐

6 Sofia likes going to the beach. ☐

DIALOGUE

3 🔊 **11.05** **Complete the conversation with the words in the list. Then listen and check.**

> poor | sorry to hear | what a shame

Alex	Hi, Naomi. What seems to be the problem?
Naomi	It's about Chris, my brother.
Alex	What about him?
Naomi	He's in hospital.
Alex	I'm ¹_____ that, Naomi. What happened?
Naomi	He broke his leg.
Alex	²_____ Chris!
Naomi	Yes. We wanted to go to the concert on Sunday. Now we can't go.
Alex	³_____ .

4 **Read the situation and complete the short conversation. Use phrases from Exercise 3 to express sympathy.**

> Melissa notices that her friend Owen has a problem. She asks him about it and finds out that Owen lost his wallet on the way to the shopping centre. He lost all his money. He wanted to buy a new games controller and can't buy one now.

Melissa What seems to be the problem, Owen? You don't look very happy.

Owen _____
_____
_____
_____
_____
_____

PHRASES FOR FLUENCY → SB p.108

5 🔊 **11.06** **Read the two conversations. Replace the phrases in *italics* with the phrases in the list. Then listen and check.**

> I can't wait. | I mean | ~~I suppose so.~~
> Tell you what. | Wait and see. | Whatever.

Conversation 1

Andy Looks like it'll start raining pretty soon.

Lexi ⁰*I think perhaps you're right.*

Andy ¹*I really don't care.* I've got so much work to do, so I can't go out anyway.

Lexi ²*Here's what I think.* I could help you, and then we could go out together. ³*What I want to say is,* if that's OK with you, of course.

Conversation 2

Grady ⁴*I'm very excited.* If the weather's OK on Saturday, we're going to go climbing. The mountain we want to climb is 3,560 metres high!

Anne Wow. That's a long way to climb! Do you think you'll get to the top?

Grady ⁵*We'll find out soon!*

0 _____*I suppose so.*_____

1 _____

2 _____

3 _____

4 _____

5 _____

A2 Key for Schools

1 Your friend, Morgan, is ill and didn't go to school this week. You want to go and see your friend.

Write a message to Morgan. In your message:
- say you are sorry that Morgan is ill
- offer to visit
- ask how you can help

Write 25 words or more.

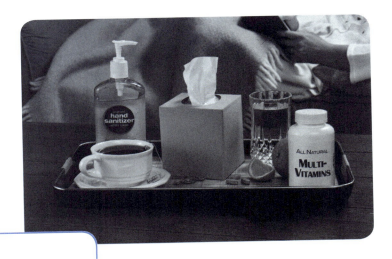

EXAM GUIDE: READING AND WRITING PART 6

In A2 Key for Schools Reading and Writing Part 6, you have to write a short message using at least 25 words.

There is a sentence to explain the situation and three items of information you must include in your message.

- Read the information about the situation very carefully.
- Read the three points you must include in the message. Make sure you write about all three points, not just one or two.
- Before you start writing, think about what you are going to say.
- What verb tenses do you need to use? Past, present or future?
- Make sure you start and finish your message correctly.
- The message is to a friend, so use friendly, informal language.
- You must write a minimum of 25 words, but you can write more, if you have time.

2 Your friend Sam wants to start running every day. You want to join your friend. Write a message to Sam. In your message:
- ask if you can go running with Sam
- recommend a good place to go running
- suggest a time to meet

Write 25 words or more.

12 TRAVEL THE WORLD

Grammar rap!
▶35

G GRAMMAR
Present perfect simple → SB p.112

1 ★☆☆ Find eleven more past participles in the puzzle. Use the irregular verb list on page 128 to help you.

R	D	S	L	E	P	T	S	F
T	O	W	S	L	E	E	P	L
A	N	U	V	U	M	S	O	E
K	E	M	S	E	E	N	K	W
E	B	W	R	I	T	T	E	N
N	O	W	R	O	T	E	N	A
A	U	F	L	O	W	N	G	R
S	G	W	A	N	O	R	O	N
T	H	D	G	O	N	E	E	O
O	T	H	E	R	T	A	S	D

0 buy	_bought_	6 sleep	_____
1 do	_____	7 speak	_____
2 fly	_____	8 swim	_____
3 go	_____	9 take	_____
4 meet	_____	10 win	_____
5 see	_____	11 write	_____

2 ★★☆ Complete the sentences with the past participles in Exercise 1.

0 I have never _____flown_____ in a plane.

1 My brother has _____ to a football match.

2 You don't want to watch that film – you've _____ it hundreds of times!

3 I'm having a great holiday. I've _____ hundreds of photographs!

4 She's really tired because she's _____ fifty emails today.

5 They haven't got any money left because they've _____ so many things.

6 We're really happy because we've _____ a competition.

7 The teacher's angry with us because we haven't _____ our homework.

3 ★★☆ When Jenny was 12, she wrote a list of things she wanted to do. Jenny is now 75. Write sentences about what she has and hasn't done. Use the present perfect of the verbs.

0 write a book ✓

1 see the Himalaya mountains ✓

2 fly in a hot air balloon ✗

3 meet the president ✗

4 sleep under the stars ✓

5 swim to France ✗

6 win a tennis tournament ✗

7 walk over the Golden Gate Bridge! ✓

0 _She's written a book._

1 _____

2 _____

3 _____

4 _____

5 _____

6 _____

7 _____

been to vs. *gone to* → SB p.112

4 ★★☆ Match the pictures with the sentences.

In Beijing. Call me. Love, Jim

0 He's been to China. _b_

1 He's gone to China. ☐

2 They've been to the supermarket. ☐

3 They've gone to the supermarket. ☐

Present perfect with *ever / never*

→ SB p.113

5 ★★☆ **Put the words in order to make questions and answers.**

0 **A** you / ever / a / won / Have / competition
Have you ever won a competition?

B never / I've / No, / anything / won
No, I've never won anything.

1 **A** been / Has / New York / to / ever / she
_____

B never / the US / she's / to / been / No,
_____

2 **A** you / eaten / ever / Have / food / Japanese
_____

B restaurant / been / never / No, / a Japanese / I've / to
_____

3 **A** ever / they / a helicopter / Have / flown / in
_____

B never / in / flown / they've / a helicopter or a plane / No,
_____

4 **A** your parents / Have / ever / angry with you / been
_____

B they've / angry / with me / lots of times / Yes, / been
_____

Present perfect vs. past simple

→ SB p.115

6 ★★☆ **Complete the conversations. Use the present perfect or past simple of the verbs.**

1 **A** Let's go to an Indian restaurant.

B But I ⁰_____*'ve never eaten*_____ (never/eat) Indian food before.

A No, you're wrong! You ¹_____ (eat) Indian food at my house last week.

B Really? Oh yes – you ²_____ (make) a curry! I remember now.

2 **A** My parents ³_____ (travel) to lots of places round the world.

B ⁴_____ (they/visit) China?

A Oh, yes, they ⁵_____ (go) to Beijing two years ago. They ⁶_____ (love) it there.

B They're lucky. I ⁷_____ (always/want) to go to China, but I ⁸_____ (never/have) the chance.

PRONUNCIATION
Sentence stress Go to page 121. 🎧

7 ★★★ **Complete the email. Use the present perfect or past simple of the verbs.**

Mark
markernest@thinkmail.com

Hi Mark,

It's August already! Sorry I ⁰_____*haven't written*_____ (not write) to you recently – the thing is, I ¹_____ (be) really busy in June and July!

Anyway, I've got news for you. Two important things ²_____ (happen) to me.

So, my first big news is that last week I ³_____ (go) to a party at my friend's house and I ⁴_____ (meet) a really nice girl called Joanna. We ⁵_____ (talk) the whole evening and we ⁶_____ (get) on together really well.

So that's good, eh? Only there's a problem, because at the end of the evening she ⁷_____ (ask) me to go ice skating with her. Of course I ⁸_____ (say) yes! But I ⁹_____ (never / try) ice skating before. Should I go? I don't want to look stupid, you know!

The other news is that my parents ¹⁰_____ (find) a new flat. So next month we're moving to a different part of town. ¹¹_____ (you / hear) of Milson Road? That's where we're going. Mum's really pleased because the flat's got a garden, and that's one thing she ¹²_____ (always / want). But I'll be a bit sad to leave this place because I ¹³_____ (live) here all my life.

Anyway, that's it for now. Write soon.

Andy

GET IT RIGHT!

Present perfect with *ever / never*

We use *never* when we want to say 'at no time in (my/your/his, etc.) life' and we use *ever* when we want to say 'at any time in (my/your/his, etc.) life'.

✓ I've seen 'Black Panther'. It's the best film I've *ever* seen.

✗ I've seen 'Black Panther'. It's the best film I've ~~never~~ seen.

Remember we don't use *not* and *never* together.

Circle the correct words.

0 Lindsay is the best friend I've *never* /(*ever*)had.

1 I've *never* / *ever* been to London, but I hope to go there next year.

2 I'm nervous about flying because I've *never* / *ever* been on a plane before.

3 I'm wearing my new shoes. They're the best shoes I've *never* / *ever* had.

4 I have *never* / *ever* visited Paris.

VOCABULARY
Transport and travel

→ SB p.115

1 ★☆☆ **Look at the pictures and complete the puzzle. What is the 'mystery' word?**

0: T R A M

The mystery word is _____ .

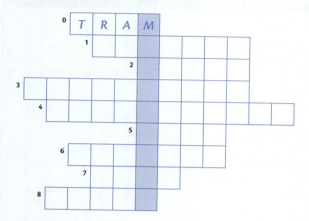

2 ★★☆ **Match the forms of transport (1–8) with the definitions (a–i).**

0	a minibus	g
1	an underground train	
2	a tram	
3	a boat	
4	a plane	
5	a bicycle	
6	a train	
7	a scooter	
8	a helicopter	

a It's like a bus but it goes on tracks.
b It's got two wheels and a small motor.
c It travels on tracks and stops at stations.
d It flies but it's smaller than a plane.
e A train that travels below the city.
f It travels on the sea, lakes and rivers.
g A small bus for about ten people.
h It's got two wheels but no motor.
i It flies and carries hundreds of people.

Travel verbs

→ SB p.115

3 ★☆☆ **Complete the sentences with the verbs in the list.**

> catch | drive | ~~flies~~ | misses | ride | take

0 Aziz is a pilot. He _____*flies*_____ A380 planes for Emirates Airlines.
1 I don't travel by car. I always _____ the train.
2 He hasn't got a car because he can't _____ .
3 She is always at the station ten minutes before her train leaves. She never _____ it.
4 Every weekend they _____ their motorbikes all the way to Scotland.
5 Please don't be late! We must _____ the 10.30 train.

4 ★★☆ **Complete the sentences. Use the correct form of the travel verbs in Exercise 3.**

0 Last year we _*flew*_ from London to Los Angeles.
1 Sometimes I'm late for school because I _____ the bus.
2 My mum _____ me to school every day – in her twenty-year-old car!
3 We never _____ our bikes when it rains. We catch the bus.
4 Are you going to _____ the 10 o'clock train?
5 When they got back to the airport, they _____ a taxi home.

REFERENCE

Travel verbs and transport

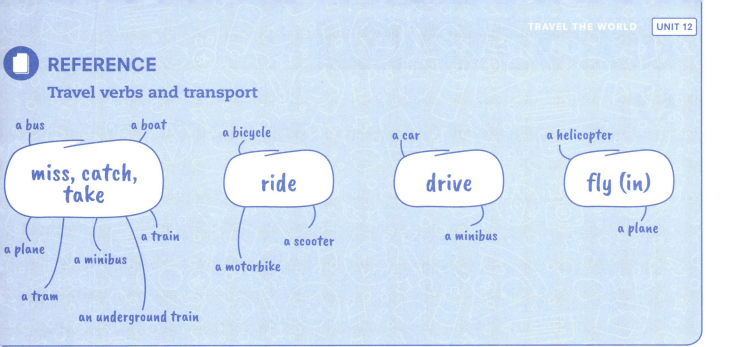

a bus
a boat

miss, catch, take

a plane
a minibus
a tram
a train
an underground train

a bicycle

ride

a motorbike
a scooter

a car

drive

a minibus

a helicopter

fly (in)

a plane

VOCABULARY *EXTRA*

1 Circle the correct words.

0 He got *in* / *on* the train in London.

1 It was raining when she got *in* / *off* the taxi.

2 You have to get *off* / *out* of the bus at the next stop.

3 We got *on* / *off* the plane and looked for our seats.

4 Are you getting *on* / *in* this train?

5 He got *on* / *in* his bike and rode to the shop.

2 Write sentences to describe the pictures.

1 He's _____

2 She's _____

3 They're _____

4 They're _____

The two travellers

One evening, an old man was sitting on a bench on the top of a hill. He was looking down at the town where he lived in the valley below him.

Just then, a traveller walked up to him – a man carrying a stick with a small bag on it containing his possessions. He stopped beside the old man to talk to him.

'Excuse me, sir,' the traveller said. 'I am going to the town down there, the town in the valley. Do you know it?'

'Yes,' said the old man. 'I know it.'

'Well,' said the traveller. 'Can you tell me – what are the people like in that town?'

The old man thought for a bit. Then he said, 'Tell me – what were the people like in the last town you were in?'

'Oh,' said the traveller. 'They were awful – horrible people. They didn't like me, and I didn't like them.'

And the old man said, 'I'm sorry to tell you that the people in the town in the valley are horrible, too. You won't like them.'

'OK,' said the traveller. And he walked away. He didn't go to the town in the valley.

About an hour later, another traveller arrived near the old man.

'Excuse me, sir,' the second traveller said. 'I am going to the town down there, the town in the valley. Do you know it?'

'Yes,' said the old man. 'I know it.'

'Well,' said the second traveller. 'Can you tell me – what are the people like in that town?'

The old man thought for a bit. Then he said, 'Tell me – what were the people like in the last town you were in?'

'Oh,' said the second traveller. 'They were wonderful – really nice people. They liked me, and I loved them.'

And the old man said, 'I'm happy to tell you that the people in the town in the valley are wonderful, too. I'm sure you'll like them very much.'

'Oh, thank you!' said the second traveller. And he walked happily down to the town in the valley.

READING

1 **Read the story and answer the questions.**

1 What question do the two travellers ask the old man?

_____

2 Which two words does the old man use to describe the people in his town?

_____

2 **Read the story again and answer the questions.**

0 What was the old man looking at when he was on the bench?

He was looking at the town where he lived.

1 What did the first traveller say about the people in the last town he visited?

_____

2 What did the first traveller decide to do after the old man's reply?

_____

3 What did the second traveller say about the people in the last town he visited?

_____

4 Where did the second traveller go when he left the old man?

_____

3 CRITICAL THINKING **What does the story tell us? Choose A, B or C.**

A When we travel to different places, we will meet all kinds of different people.

B Being warm and friendly changes the experiences we have with people.

C Before we visit a place, it's a good idea to ask questions about the people who live there.

4 **What do you think people should do when they visit new countries? Number the activities in order of importance for you.**

☐ Find out about the culture before going

☐ Go to local events

☐ Learn some phrases in the local language

☐ Speak to local people

☐ Meet other travellers

☐ Try the local food

☐ Visit famous tourist attractions

DEVELOPING *Writing*

An essay

1 **INPUT** **Read the advertisement for a competition in a magazine and complete the notes.**

1 The competition is for young _____ .
2 The general topic of the essay is _____ .
3 The prize is _____ .

CALLING ALL YOUNG

TRAVEL WRITERS!

We want to hear about your travel experiences and plans – and YOU could win a prize!

Send us an essay about your travels:

- some places you have been to
- the best trip you have made – when and where did you go, and what did you do?
- a place you want to visit – why?

We'll publish the top three essays on our website and the winner will receive a digital camera!

2 **Read Rebecca's essay for the competition. Underline the information that the advertisement asks for in the essay.**

1 I haven't travelled a lot outside my country, but I've had some great holidays with my family. We've driven through the amazing countryside in the north, and we've gone skiing a few times in the mountains.

2 But the best trip I've ever had was when we travelled to the south of France last summer.
We flew to Paris, and the next day we caught the train to Avignon – the fastest train I've ever been on! During our week in Avignon, we explored the old city and took buses to some of the villages up in the hills. Also our hotel organised a minibus to take us to the coast. It was beautiful there, so I was sad when we had to leave.

3 Now I can't wait to go travelling again. My dream is to go to China because it looks so exciting and so different from my country.

3 **ANALYSE** **Read the essay again and complete the sentences with the number of the paragraph.**

0 Paragraph _3_ is about Rebecca's hopes for the future.
1 Paragraph __ introduces the topic of travelling.
2 Paragraph __ describes a particular set of events in the past.
3 Paragraph __ is about some of the travel experiences Rebecca has had in her life.
4 Paragraph __ explains why she wants to travel to a certain place.
5 Paragraph __ contains the most information.

 WRITING TIP: an essay

- Use quite formal language in an essay.
- Organise the essay into paragraphs:
  - Start with a short introduction to the topic.
  - Give more detailed information in the main part of the essay.
  - Finish with a short conclusion or an explanation for something.
- Before you start writing, make a plan.

4 **PLAN** **Read the competition advert again and plan your essay. Think about the different tenses you need to use in the three parts of the essay.**

Paragraph 1	
Paragraph 2	
Paragraph 3	

5 **PRODUCE** **Now, use your notes in Exercise 4 to write your essay in 120–150 words.**

🎧 LISTENING

ATLANTIC OCEAN

North Sea

Irish Sea

Celtic Sea

London
Margate

English Channel

1 🔊 12.02 **Listen to part of a radio phone–in programme and choose the correct words.**

1 Ross Edgley is *sailing / swimming* round the coast of Britain.

2 At the moment, he's in *Scotland / England*.

3 He's doing the trip *on his own / with a team*.

4 So far, the weather has *sometimes / never* been bad.

2 🔊 12.02 **Listen again and circle. Choose the correct answer A, B or C.**

0 How did Jacob find out about this story?

  A He met Ross Edgley.

  B He saw a video about it.

  C He heard it on the news.

1 Where is Ross now?

  A Near the end of his journey

  B In the middle of his journey

  C 200 kilometres from the start of his journey

2 How far does he swim every day?

  A About 30 kilometres

  B About 6 kilometres

  C About 150 kilometres

3 During the trip, Ross hasn't

  A slept on the boat.

  B eaten much food.

  C walked on land.

4 Ross has had a problem with

  A his tongue.

  B his team.

  C his toe.

DIALOGUE

3 🔊 12.03 **Match Jacob's answers with Tina's questions. There are two extra questions. Then listen and check.**

  a Does he swim every day?

  b How far has he swum?

  c Does he have to eat special food?

  d Do you know anything else about the trip?

  e Has he had any problems so far?

  f How long will the swim take?

  g Has he seen any sharks?

  h How far does he have to swim every day?

1 Jacob	About 150 days. He started in June and he should finish in November.	☐
2 Jacob	About 30 kilometres.	☐
3 Jacob	Well, I know that he isn't alone. He's got a team of people to help him.	☐
4 Jacob	Yes. He swims for six hours, then he returns to the boat for six hours to eat and sleep.	☐
5 Jacob	No, he doesn't, but he has to eat a lot of food because he gets hungry.	☐
6 Jacob	Well, there's been some bad weather, like very strong winds and storms.	☐

Train to TH!NK

Exploring differences

4 Look at the table. Are the sentences true about only waiters, only taxi drivers, or both? Tick (✓) the correct column.

You ...	waiters	taxi drivers	both
meet a lot of people.			✓
spend a long time on your feet.			
have to carry things.			
can work in any weather.			
have to remember things.			
wear special clothes.			

5 Think about houses and flats. What things are the same? What things are different? Write three more things in the left-hand column. Tick (✓) the correct column.

It ...	house	flat	both
has got bedrooms.			✓

A2 Key for Schools

1 For these questions, choose the correct answer.

> **This week we're interviewing Leila Moreton, a travel journalist. She tells us about her job ...**
>
> I've got the best job ever. I'm a journalist and I write about activity holidays for teenagers. I travel to new places to experience different holidays. Then, I write articles for travel magazines and websites.
>
> **Tell us about some of your experiences, Leila.**
>
> I've been sailing in Greece and I've been kayaking in Canada – not on holiday, but as research for my job! It isn't only about adventure – I've also learnt to make a video, how to cook and do circus skills! There are holidays for every interest.
>
> **How did you find your dream job?**
>
> Well, I've always loved writing. English was my best subject at school and I wrote for our school website. I also love travelling. When I was a child, we lived in South Africa for a few years because of my parents' jobs. It was a great opportunity to explore new places. When I finished school, I worked for a travel company and that's when I got interested in teen activity holidays. My job is perfect because I do my two favourite things: writing and travelling. I don't need holidays! In fact, I usually stay at home for my holidays because travel is work for me.
>
> **Have you enjoyed everything you've done?**
>
> Not everything! My job's fun, but I've discovered that I don't like riding horses or camels, and I'm frightened of flying in small planes and helicopters!

1 What does Leila do?
   A She's a travel agent.
   B She's a school teacher.
   C She's a travel writer.

2 Leila's interested in
   A exciting holidays.
   B learning new sports.
   C learning skills for work.

3 When Leila was a child, she
   A never went on holiday.
   B lived in a different country.
   C didn't speak English.

4 In her holidays, she
   A visits new places.
   B doesn't go away.
   C goes horse-riding.

5 Leila says she has
   A always had lots of fun.
   B never liked flying in planes.
   C learnt two things about herself.

EXAM GUIDE: READING AND WRITING PART 3

In A2 Key for Schools Reading and Writing Part 3, you have to read a short article and then answer five multiple-choice questions.

- First, read the article carefully. Don't worry about words you don't understand. Focus on the general meaning.
- Look at the first question and find the part of the text that it refers to.
- Read all the options carefully.
- Re-read the part of the text and choose the correct answer.
- You won't see the same words in the questions and the article, so look out for words and expressions that have the same meaning.
- The questions are always in the same order as the text.

CONSOLIDATION

🎧 LISTENING

1 🔊 **12.04** **Listen to the conversation. Choose the correct answer A, B or C.**

1 What happened to William?
   A He fell off his bike and hurt his shoulder.
   B He fell off his motorbike and hurt his back.
   C He fell off his motorbike and hurt his shoulder.

2 What does William think is dangerous?
   A driving in traffic
   B riding a bicycle
   C riding a motorbike

3 How does William usually get to work now?
   A by motorbike
   B by car
   C by bus

2 🔊 **12.04** **Listen again and answer the questions.**

0 When did William buy his motorbike?
   He bought it two weeks ago.

1 Why did he buy a motorbike?
   _____

2 Why doesn't he want to use the underground?
   _____

3 When will William get on his motorbike again?
   _____

4 What does he like about going to work by bus?
   _____

3 **Complete the sentences with *been* or *gone*.**

Tom Your dad travels a lot. Where is he this time?
Alice He's ⁰____*gone*____ to Brazil.
Tom Lucky him! Have you ever ¹_____ to Brazil?
Alice No, I haven't. I've never ²_____ anywhere outside Europe.
Tom Where's your sister by the way?
Alice She's ³_____ to the dentist's with my mum.
Tom I haven't ⁴_____ to the dentist's for a long time.

⊚ GRAMMAR

4 **Complete the conversations with the present perfect of the verbs.**

0 A Where's Martin?
   B I don't know. I *haven't seen* (not see) him today.

1 A Are Sam and Julia here?
   B No, they _____ (go) to the cinema.

2 A Is there any food in the kitchen?
   B No – my brother _____ (eat) it all!

3 A _____ (you / write) to your aunt?
   B Not yet. I'll do it tonight.

4 A Are you enjoying Los Angeles?
   B It's great. I _____ (meet) lots of nice people.

5 A Have you got a lot of homework?
   B No, only a little – and I _____ (do) it all!

6 A Is this a good book?
   B I don't know. I _____ (not read) it.

7 A Why are you so happy?
   B My parents _____ (give) me a new bike for my birthday!

🄰𝗓 VOCABULARY

5 **Complete the words.**

0 Can we watch this film? I haven't s*e* *e* *n* it before, but everyone says it's great.

1 Some really rich people fly between cities by h_ _ _ _ _ _ _ _ _ _.

2 He can't walk now because he's broken his a_ _ _ _ _.

3 In some European cities you can still see t_ _ _s that travel around the streets.

4 He looked really bored, with his e_ _ _ _ _s on the table and his head between his hands.

5 Wow! It's my first time on a plane! I've never f_ _ _ _ _ before today!

6 We were late, so we didn't c_ _ _ _ _ the train.

7 The dog was really hot – its t_ _ _ _ _ _ was hanging out of its mouth.

6 Circle the correct words.

Jake Hi, Mum. I've ⁰*been*/ *gone* into town – and look!
I've ¹*buy* / *bought* a new shirt.

Mum It's nice, Jake. But isn't it a bit small? You're tall
and you've got big ²*shoulders* / *ankles*.

Jake No, Mum, it's fine. I think ³*I wear* / *I'll wear* it to
Evie's party on Saturday.

Mum Oh, is she having a party?

Jake Yes, it's for her birthday. ⁴*She's invited* / *She
invites* everyone from school.

Mum But her birthday ⁵*was* / *has been* last month!

Jake I know. But her mother was ill, so she couldn't
have a party then.

Mum Oh, I'm sorry to ⁶*know* / *hear* that. Is her mother
OK now?

Jake Oh, yes, she's ⁷*being* / *doing* OK. She had a
problem with her ⁸*stomach* / *knee* – the doctors
think she ⁹*ate* / *has eaten* something bad.

Mum Oh, ¹⁰*sorry* / *poor* Evie. Well, please tell her that
I hope the party is great.

Jake Thanks, Mum. I'll tell her when I ¹¹*see* / *will see* her.

DIALOGUE

7 🔊 12.05 **Complete the conversation with words
from the list. There are two that you don't need.**

> as soon as | ~~been~~ | doing | gone | hear | if
> knee | poor | shame | went | will | won't

Harvey Hi, Amber. Where have you ⁰ _been_ ?

Amber At the doctor's. I hurt my ¹_____ the
other day.

Harvey Oh, I'm sorry to ²_____ that. Is everything
OK now?

Amber Not really. I'll have to see him again ³_____
it doesn't get better.

Harvey ⁴_____ you.

Amber Oh, it's not so bad. It hurts a bit, but I'm
⁵_____ OK. Listen, I'm looking for Matt.
Do you know where he is?

Harvey Oh, he isn't here. He's ⁶_____ to see his
grandmother. She's ill. He ⁷_____ be back
until about six o'clock.

Amber That's a ⁸_____ . I really want to talk to him.
Can you ask him to call me, please?

Harvey Sure. I'll ask him ⁹_____ he gets back.

📖 READING

8 **Read the text about children and schools in Niger.
Answer the questions.**

0 In Niger, what percentage of people have running
water at home?
20% of people have running water at home.

1 Who often goes to get water for a family?
_____

2 Why is Sani often two hours late for school?
_____

3 Why does Badjeba sometimes fall asleep in lessons?
_____

4 Why do families send children to get water when it
makes them late for school?
_____

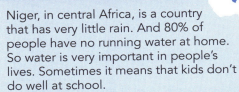

School or water?

Niger, in central Africa, is a country
that has very little rain. And 80% of
people have no running water at home.
So water is very important in people's
lives. Sometimes it means that kids don't
do well at school.

Children are often the ones who have to find water
for the family. They go out on donkeys and travel
up to ten kilometres to get water. And then they
are late for school, or they don't go at all. Sani, 11,
gets water for his family in the morning and usually
gets to school at 10 o'clock – two hours late. 'Some
of the other children are lucky,' he says. 'They don't
have to get water and so they learn more quickly
than me.'

It's hard for the children to study. One girl, Badjeba,
says, 'I get up at 4.30 to get water, five kilometres
away. Then I take it home. Then I walk to school.
I'm exhausted. I'm so tired that I fall asleep in the
lessons. And after school, I have to go and find
water again.'

In one classroom, the teacher asks: 'How many
of you were late today because you had to get
water?' And about 90% of the kids put their hand
up. Their families send them to get water – school is
important but water is life.

✏️ WRITING

9 **Imagine you are either Sani or Badjeba. Write
a diary entry for a school day (about 100–120
words). Write about these things.**

- what you did before school
- what you did at school
- what you did after school

PRONUNCIATION

UNIT 1
Plurals and third person verb endings: /s/, /z/ or /ɪz/

1 Add -s or -es to the present simple verbs. Write them in the correct column.

> cook | dance | enjoy | finish | give
> need | play | relax | sleep | swim
> take | want | wash | watch | write

/s/ – works	/z/ – lives	/ɪz/ – closes
cooks		

2  🔊 1.01 **Listen, check and repeat.**

3 Complete the sentences with the plural nouns.

> bikes | blogs | buses | cats
> players | puzzles | quizzes | stamps

0 Jane enjoys writing cooking and sports _blogs_ . /z/

1 Julie's favourite games are crosswords and _____ . /z/

2 Luke's got lots of pets – a dog, some fish and four black and white _____ . /s/

3 The girls in that team are all good _____ . /z/

4 Julie watches _____ on TV. /ɪz/

5 Many students like riding their _____ in the park. /s/

6 Jenny catches the red _____ in London. /ɪz/

7 Lewis collects _____ and bottle tops. /s/

4 🔊 1.02 **Listen, check and repeat.**

UNIT 2
Contractions

1 Match the rhyming words.

0 I'm	**a** here
1 she's	**b** time
2 they're	**c** chair
3 it's	**d** please
4 we're	**e** sits

2 🔊 2.01 **Listen, check and repeat.**

3 Now match these rhyming words.

0 who's	**a** door
1 we've	**b** years
2 let's	**c** choose
3 you're	**d** gets
4 here's	**e** leave

4 🔊 2.02 **Listen, check and repeat.**

UNIT 3
Vowel sounds: /ɪ/ and /iː/

1 🔊 3.04 **Put your finger on *Start*. Listen to the words. Go up if you hear the /ɪ/ sound and down if you hear the /iː/ sound. Say the name. You'll hear the words twice.**

0 _____ _Pete_
1 _____
2 _____
3 _____
4 _____
5 _____

2 🔊 3.05 **Listen, check and repeat.**

UNIT 4
-er /ə/ at the end of words

1 **Complete the sentences with the words in the list.**

> after | answer | daughter | father
> ~~later~~ | other | paper | writer

0 Ten minutes _____*later*_____ an ambulance was there.

1 My friend Sara wants to be a _____ .

2 I don't know the _____ to that question.

3 Our teacher always asks us to speak to each
_____ in English.

4 Please write your answers on a separate piece of
_____ .

5 That little girl over there is Mr Power's
_____ .

6 My _____ 's a farmer. He works very hard.

7 Can you come to my house _____ school?

2 🔊 **4.01** **Listen, check and repeat.**

UNIT 5
Regular past tense endings

1 **How many syllables are there? Write them in the columns.**

> ~~asked~~ | closed | missed | ~~needed~~ | played
> rested | shouted | started | tried | wanted

one syllable /d/ or /t/	two syllables /ɪd/
asked	needed

2 🔊 **5.01** **Listen, check and repeat.**

3 **Circle the correct words to complete the rule.**

The -ed endings of regular verbs in the past simple are
¹*pronounced as a separate syllable / not pronounced as
a separate syllable*, /ɪd/, when the infinitive form of the
verb ends in /t/ or /d/ only.
In all other cases, the -ed endings are ²*pronounced as a
separate syllable / not pronounced as a separate syllable*,
but as /t/ or /d/.

4 **Write the words ending in the /t/ and /d/ sounds in the correct column.**

> ~~carried~~ | ~~cooked~~ | enjoyed | finished | helped
> loved | stayed | tried | washed | worked

/t/ – asked	/d/ – closed
cooked	carried

5 🔊 **5.02** **Listen, check and repeat.**

UNIT 6
Stressed syllables in words

1 **Write the words in the correct columns.**

> ~~adventurous~~ | confident | friendly | good
> helpful | intelligent | interesting | nice

1 One syllable	2 Two syllables
_____	_____
_____	_____

3 Three syllables	4 Four syllables
_____	adventurous
_____	_____

2 🔊 **6.01** **Listen, check and repeat.**

3 **Which syllable is stressed? Write the words in the correct columns.**

> adventurous | ~~confident~~ | disappointed
> easy-going | important | intelligent
> interesting | relaxing

1 Ooo	2 oOo
confident	_____
_____	_____

3 oOoo	4 ooOo
_____	_____
_____	_____

4 🔊 **6.02** **Listen, check and repeat.**

UNIT 7
Vowel sounds: /ʊ/ and /uː/

1 🔊 7.04 **What are you buying? Put your finger on Start. Listen to the words. Go up if you hear the /ʊ/ sound and down if you hear the /uː/ sound. Say the word at the end. You'll hear the words twice.**

books = /ʊ/

START

zoo = /uː/

/ʊ/ footballs
/uː/ fruit
/ʊ/ books
/uː/ boots
/ʊ/ sugar
/uː/ shoes
/ʊ/ cookers
/uː/ soup

0 _____*Boots*_____
1 _____
2 _____
3 _____
4 _____
5 _____

2 🔊 7.05 **Listen, check and repeat.**

3 **All of these words are written with the letters *oo* but they are not pronounced in the same way. Write each word in the /ʊ/ or /uː/ column.**

choose | cook | cool | food
good | ~~look~~ | school | stood

/ʊ/ – foot	/uː/ – room
look	

4 a **Which words rhyme with *should*?**
   _____ and _____ .

  b **Which word rhymes with *shoes*?** _____ .

5 🔊 7.06 **Listen, check and repeat.**

UNIT 8
Strong and weak forms of *was* and *were*

1 **Write *was*, *wasn't*, *were* or *weren't* to complete the sentences.**

  1 A ____*Was*____ she happy to get her new bike?
    B Yes, she _____ . She loves it.
  2 A _____ they playing volleyball in the park?
    B No, they _____ . They _____ at the beach.
  3 A Look – that girl _____ at the pool yesterday.
    B No, she _____ !
    A Yes, she _____ ! She's a good swimmer.
    B She _____ . The girl we saw had long brown hair.
  4 A They _____ very happy with the restaurant last night.
    B Really? Why not?
    A Because they _____ waiting for their food for a long time.
  5 A _____ you at the football match last night?
    B No, I _____ . I _____ studying for an exam.
    A _____ you? So was I!

2 🔊 8.01 **Listen, check and repeat.**

3 **Circle the stressed forms of these verbs.**

4 🔊 8.01 **Listen again and check.**

UNIT 9
Vowel sounds: /ɪ/ and /aɪ/

1 **Write the words in the columns.**

find | fine | ~~give~~ | gym | list | nice | night
sing | smile | spring | style | thin | wild | wish

/ɪ/ – think	/aɪ/ – drive
give	

2 🔊 9.01 **Listen, check and repeat.**

3 **Match to make sentences.**

  0 I'm going to Keep Fit   a driving at night.
  1 Kim doesn't like   b has a healthy lifestyle.
  2 Lions and tigers   c ride our bikes.
  3 Mike exercises and   d classes at the gym.
  4 It's a nice day, so let's   e are happier in the wild.

4 🔊 9.02 **Listen and check.**

5 (Circle) all of the words in the sentences with the /aɪ/ sound.

6 🔊 9.03 Listen, check and repeat.

UNIT 10
Voiced /ð/ and unvoiced /θ/ consonants

1 Complete the sentences.

> clothes | Earth | Maths | months | then
> ~~things~~ | think | third | Thursday | youth

0 There are so many _things_ to do in Sydney.

1 Let's go shopping. I want to buy some new _____ .

2 These three students came first, second and _____ in the race.

3 My father's birthday's on _____ .

4 We had dinner and _____ we went to the theatre.

5 I _____ we should go out to a restaurant tonight.

6 We must look after the _____ ; it's a beautiful planet.

7 There are twelve _____ in a year.

8 We've got a _____ class after the break.

9 A _____ is a young person.

2 🔊 10.03 Listen, check and repeat.

3 (Circle) all the words in the sentences with a voiced *th* sound. Underline all the words with an unvoiced *th* sound.

UNIT 11
The /h/ consonant sound

1 Complete the sentences with the words in the list.

> hair | happy | healthy | hear | help
> here | ~~homework~~ | hospital | humans | hurt

0 I'll come to your house when I've finished my History _homework_ .

1 It's _____ to eat honey.

2 Harry had to go to the _____ in an ambulance.

3 That suitcase looks heavy. Can I _____ you carry it?

4 Helen's got beautiful long black _____ .

5 I couldn't _____ the music because the headphones weren't working.

6 I hope you'll be _____ in your new home.

7 In the future _____ won't have as much hair as they do now.

8 Hilary _____ her knee while she was running yesterday.

9 Can you come _____ and help me, please?

2 🔊 11.01 Listen, check and repeat.

UNIT 12
Sentence stress

1 Complete the sentences.

> cooker | eggs | English | farmer
> island | laptop | ~~scarf~~ | taxi

0 I'm wearing a <u>shirt</u>, a <u>skirt</u>, a <u>hat</u> and a _scarf_ .

1 An artist, a doctor, a teacher and a _____ .

2 We've got Maths, then Art, then History and then _____ .

3 We need a desk, a lamp, a sofa and a _____ .

4 We caught a plane and then a train and then a bus and then a _____ .

5 We put in flour and sugar and then butter and _____ .

6 For sale: a digital camera, a pen drive, a microphone and a _____ .

7 We saw a lake, a river, a jungle and an _____ .

2 🔊 12.01 Listen, check and repeat.

3 Underline the stressed words in the lists in Exercise 1.

4 🔊 12.01 Listen again, check and repeat.

5 Look at the stressed words in the sentences 0–7. Then read and (circle) the correct word to complete the rule.

> We generally stress words like [1]*nouns / articles* that give us information. We don't generally stress words like [2]*nouns / articles*.

GRAMMAR REFERENCE

UNIT 1
Present simple

1   **We use the present simple for actions that happen repeatedly or habitually.**

   *Paul often **goes** to the cinema.*
   *We **have** dinner at 8.00 every evening.*

   We also use the present simple for things that are always or normally true.

   *The sun **comes up** in the east.*
   *We **go** to a big school in London.*

2   **With most subjects, the present simple is the same as the base form of the verb. However, with a third person singular subject (*he, she, it*), the verb has an –s ending.**

   *I **play** tennis on Saturdays.*
   *She **plays** tennis on Saturdays.*

   If a verb ends with –sh, –ch, –ss or –x, we add –es.

   he watches, she catches, he misses, she fixes

   If a verb ends with consonant + –y, we change the –y to –i and add –es.

   she studies, he worries

   If a verb ends with vowel + –y, then it is regular.
   play ➜ plays, say ➜ says, buy ➜ buys

3   **The negative of the present simple is formed with *don't* (*do not*) or *doesn't* (*does not*) + base form of the verb.**

   *I **don't like** carrots.   She **doesn't like** carrots.*

4   **Present simple questions and short answers are formed with *do* or *does*.**

   Do *you* **like** *cats?*   *Yes, I **do**. / No, I **don't**.*
   Does *Jo* **live** *here?*   *Yes, she **does**. / No, she **doesn't**.*

like + -ing

1   **After verbs which express likes and dislikes we often use verb + –ing.**

   *We **love watching** films at home.*
   *My sister **enjoys reading** travel books.*

2   **If a verb ends in –e, we drop the –e before adding –ing.**

   live ➜ living   ride ➜ riding

   If a short verb ends in consonant + vowel + consonant, we double the final consonant before adding –ing.

   get ➜ getting, shop ➜ shopping, travel ➜ travelling

UNIT 2
Present continuous

1   **We use the present continuous for actions that are happening now or around the time of speaking.**

   *My friends and I **are playing** an online game at the moment.*
   *It's **raining** now.*

2   **The present continuous is formed with the present simple of *be* + verb + –ing.**

   *I'm **listening** to music.   I'm **not listening** to music.*
   *You're **walking** very fast!   You **aren't walking** very fast.*
   *Alison is **talking** to Jo.   Alison **isn't talking** to Jo.*

3   **The question is formed with the present simple of *be* + subject + verb + –ing. Short answers are formed using *Yes/No* + pronoun + the correct form of *be* (positive or negative).**

   Is *Susanna* **eating**?   *Yes, she **is**. / No, she **isn't**.*
   Are *the boys* **having** *fun?*   *Yes, they **are**. / No, they **aren't**.*
   *What **are** you **doing**?   Why **is** she **crying**?*

Verbs of perception

Verbs of perception (*taste / smell / look / sound*) are not used in the present continuous when they are used to give an opinion. They are used in the present simple only.

*This juice **doesn't taste** very nice.*
*Mmm! The food **smells** fantastic!*
*These trousers **don't look** very good on me.*
*I don't know who the singer is, but she **sounds** wonderful.*

Present simple vs. present continuous

1   **We use different time expressions with the present simple and the present continuous.**

   Present simple: *every day, on Mondays, at the weekend, usually, sometimes, often, never*
   Present continuous: *today, right now, at the moment*
   *James **usually walks** to school, but today he's **taking** the bus.*

2   **Some verbs aren't normally used in the continuous form. They are called *state verbs* or *stative verbs* because they talk about a state, not an action. Here are some common examples:**

   believe, know, understand, remember, want, need, mean, like, hate
   *I **believe** you. He **knows** a lot about music.*
   *Morgan **wants** to have dinner now.*

UNIT 3
Countable and uncountable nouns

1 Nouns in English are countable or uncountable.

Countable nouns have both singular and plural forms, for example:

bicycle ➜ *bicycles*, *school* ➜ *schools*, *man* ➜ *men*

But uncountable nouns do not have a plural form. They are always singular, for example:

food, music, money, rice, bread, information

2 Countable nouns can take singular or plural verbs.

That car is Japanese.   Those cars are Japanese.
That woman works with me.
Those women work with my mum.

Uncountable nouns always take singular verbs.

This food is horrible.   The music is too loud!

a / an; some / any

1 With singular countable nouns, we can use *a / an* to talk about a specific thing or person.

They've got a car.   She's eating an orange.

2 With plural countable nouns, we use *some* (positive) or *any* (negative).

I want to buy some apples.   We haven't got any eggs.

3 With uncountable nouns, we don't use *a / an* – we use *some / any*, like plural countable nouns.

Let's listen to some music. I don't want any food.

4 We use *some* to talk about an unspecified number or amount. We normally use *some* in positive sentences.

He bought some fruit in town.

We often use *some* in requests and offers.

Can I have some orange juice, please?
Do you want some cheese?

5 We use *any* to talk about an unspecified number or amount. We normally use *any* in negative sentences, and in questions.

He didn't buy any fruit.   Is there any fruit in the kitchen?

How much and (how) many; a lot of / lots of

1 We use *many* with plural countable nouns and *much* with uncountable nouns.

Countable
She doesn't eat many vegetables.
How many children have they got?

Uncountable
He doesn't eat much fruit.   How much time have we got?

2 We usually use *many* and *much* in negative sentences and questions.

I don't go to many concerts.
How many eggs do you want?

3 In positive sentences, we normally use *a lot of* or *lots of*. *A lot of / lots of* can be used with plural countable nouns and with uncountable nouns.

Chris has got a lot of / lots of DVDs.
You can get a lot of / lots of on the Internet.

too much / too many / not enough + noun

1 We use *too many* with plural countable nouns, and *too much* with uncountable nouns.

There are too many chairs in the room.
There's too much salt in my food.

2 We use *not enough* with plural countable nouns and with uncountable nouns to say that we think more is / are needed.

There aren't enough chairs in the room.
There isn't enough salt in my food.

too + adjective / (not) + adjective + enough

1 We use *too* + adjective to say that it's more than we like or want.

This soup is too hot.   The clothes are too expensive.

2 We use (*not*) + adjective + *enough* to say that something is less than we like or want.

This bag isn't big enough to put everything in.

UNIT 4
Possessive adjectives

1 Here is the list of possessive adjectives:

my, your, his, her, its, our, their

2 We use possessive adjectives to say who something belongs to.

My name's Jack.   Is he your brother?
Look at his hair!   Her bike is really expensive.
The DVD isn't in its box. They love their cat.

Possessive pronouns

1 Here is the list of possessive pronouns:

mine, yours, his, hers, ours, theirs

2 Possessive pronouns can take the place of possessive adjective + noun.

Is this your book / yours? No, it isn't my book / mine.
I like her hair, but I don't like his.

Whose

When we want to ask a question about who the owner of something is, we use the word *whose*. There are two possible constructions after *whose*.

Whose book is this? or *Whose* is this book?

Possessive 's

1 **To talk about possession we can add 's to the end of a name / noun.**

   Annie's bike is really fantastic.
   That's my *brother's* bedroom.

2 **If the name / noun ends in an -s (for example, plural nouns), we add the apostrophe (') after the final -s.**

   That's our *neighbours'* dog.
   I don't like *James'* shirt.

Past simple of *be* (was / were)

1 **We use the past simple to talk about actions and events in the past.**

2 **The past simple of *be* is *was / wasn't* or *were / weren't*.**

   I *was* at school yesterday.   You *were* late yesterday.
   My sister *wasn't* there.   The DVDs *weren't* very good.

3 **Questions with *was / were* are formed by putting the verb before the subject.**

   Were you at school yesterday?   *Was* Maria with you?

UNIT 5
Past simple: regular verbs (positive and negative)

1 **In the past simple, regular verbs have an -ed ending. The form is the same for all subjects.**

   I *walked* to the park.   You *played* well yesterday.
   Carla *opened* the window.

   If a verb ends in -e, we add only -d.

   like ➡ liked   hate ➡ hated   use ➡ used

   If a verb ends with consonant + -y, we change the -y to -i and add -ed.

   study ➡ studied   try ➡ tried   marry ➡ married

   If a short verb ends in consonant + vowel + consonant, we double the final consonant before adding -ed.

   stop ➡ stopped   plan ➡ planned   travel ➡ travelled

   If a short verb ends in consonant + vowel + -y, it is regular.

   play ➡ played   stay ➡ stayed

2 **The past simple negative is formed with *didn't* (*did not*) + base form of the verb. The form is the same for all subjects:**

   I / We / She *didn't enjoy* the film last night.

3 **Past time expressions are often used with the past simple.**

   yesterday, yesterday morning, last night, last week, a month ago, two years ago, on Sunday

Modifiers: *very, really, quite*

1 **We use the words *very, really, quite* to say more about an adjective. The words *very* and *really* make an adjective stronger.**

   The food was good ➡ The food was *very* good.
   The film was exciting ➡ The film was *really* exciting.

2 **We often use *quite* to say 'a little bit'.**

   The room was *quite small*. (not very small, but a bit small)
   The film was *quite long*. (not very long, but a bit long)

UNIT 6
Past simple: irregular verbs

1 **A lot of common verbs are irregular. This means that the past simple form is different – they don't have the usual -ed ending.**

   go ➡ went, see ➡ saw, eat ➡ ate, think ➡ thought

2 **The form of the past simple for these verbs is the same for all persons (I / you / he / she / it / we / they).**

   See page 128 for a list of irregular verbs.

3 **The negative of irregular verbs is formed in the same way as regular verbs: *didn't* (*did not*) + base form of the verb.**

   We *didn't enjoy* the concert.
   I *didn't know* the answer to the question.

Past simple: (regular and irregular verbs) questions and short answers

1 **Past simple questions and short answers are formed with *did*. The form is the same for regular and irregular verbs.**

   Did you *talk* to Barbara this morning?
   Did you *see* that great match last night?

2 **Short answers are formed with Yes / No + pronoun + *did / didn't*.**

   Did you like the film? *Yes, I did.*
   Did she phone you last night? *No, she didn't.*

Double genitive

We use the double genitive to talk about one of many things that we have. We form it with noun + *of* + possessive pronoun (see Unit 4). We can also use noun + *of* + noun with possessive 's.

He's *a friend of mine*. (I have many friends.)
They are *neighbours of ours*. (We have many neighbours.)

UNIT 7
should / shouldn't

1   **When we want to say that something is a good idea (or is a bad idea), we can use *should* or *shouldn't*.**

    I **should study** this weekend. (I think it's a good idea.)
    They **shouldn't buy** that car. (I think it's a bad idea.)
    Should we go out tonight? (Do you think this is a good idea?)

2   ***Should* is a modal verb. We use *should* / *shouldn't* + base form of the verb, and the form is the same for all subjects. We don't use any form of *do* in the negative.**

    I **should try** to study more.
    I **shouldn't watch** TV tonight.

3   **Questions are formed with *should* + subject + base form of the verb. Again, we don't use any form of *do* in questions or short answers.**

    Should I **ask** the teacher?
    Yes, you **should**. / No, you **shouldn't**.

have to / don't have to

1   **We use *have to* to say that it is necessary or very important to do something.**

    I'm late, I **have to go** now. We **have to be** at school at 8.30.

    With a third person singular subject (*he, she, it*) we use *has to*.

    Maggie is very ill – she **has to stay** in bed.
    My dad **has to go** to York tomorrow for a meeting.

2   **We use the negative form *don't* / *doesn't have to* to say that it isn't necessary or important to do something.**

    It's Sunday, so I **don't have to get up** early.
    She isn't late – she **doesn't have to hurry**.

3   **We form questions with *do* or *does*.**

    Do I **have to go** to the dentist?
    Does he **have to go** home now?

4   **All forms of *have to* are followed by the base form of the verb.**

mustn't vs. don't have to

1   **We use *mustn't* to say that it is necessary or very important not to do something.**

    You **mustn't be** late.   I **mustn't forget** to phone Jenny.

2   ***Mustn't* has a different meaning from *don't* / *doesn't have to*.**

    You **don't have to tell** your friends. (It isn't necessary for you to tell them, but you can if you want to.)
    You **mustn't tell** your friends. (Don't tell your friends – it's a secret!)

UNIT 8
Past continuous

1   **We use the past continuous to talk about actions in progress at a certain time in the past.**

    In 2012, we **were living** in the US.
    At 4 o'clock yesterday, I **was sitting** in a lesson.
    Last night, the TV was on, but I **wasn't watching** it.

2   **The past continuous is formed with the past simple of *be* + verb + *-ing*.**

    I **was reading** a book. I **wasn't enjoying** it.
    You **were running** very fast! But you **weren't winning**!
    Jo **was playing** computer games. She **wasn't studying**.

3   **The question is formed with the past simple of *be* + subject + verb + *-ing*. Short answers are formed with Yes / No + pronoun + *was* / *were* or *wasn't* / *weren't*.**

    Was James **running**? Yes, he **was**. / No, he **wasn't**.
    What **were** you **studying**?   Why **was** she **crying**?

Past continuous vs. past simple

1   **When we talk about the past, we use the past simple for actions that happened at one particular time. We use the past continuous for background actions.**

    When Alex **arrived**, I **was having** dinner.
    He **was running** very fast and he **didn't see** the tree.

2   **We often use *when* with the past simple, and *while* with the past continuous.**

    I was reading **when** the phone **rang**.
    While my father **was running**, he fell into a river.

UNIT 9
Comparative adjectives

1   **When we want to compare two things, or two groups of things, we use a comparative form + *than*.**

    I'm **older than** my brother.
    France is **bigger than** Britain.

2   **With short adjectives, we normally add *-er*.**

    old ➡ older   cheap ➡ cheaper   clever ➡ cleverer

    If the adjective ends in *-e*, we only add *-r*.

    nice ➡ nicer   safe ➡ safer

    If the adjective ends with consonant + *-y*, we change the *-y* to *-i* and add *-er*.

    easy ➡ easier   early ➡ earlier   happy ➡ happier

    If the adjective ends in a consonant + vowel + consonant, we double the final consonant and add *-er*.

    big ➡ bigger   sad ➡ sadder   thin ➡ thinner

3 With longer adjectives (more than two syllables), we don't change the adjective – we put *more* in front of it.

expensive ➜ ***more*** *expensive*   *difficult* ➜ ***more*** *difficult*
interesting ➜ ***more*** *interesting*

4 Some adjectives are irregular – they have a different comparative form.

good ➜ ***better***   *bad* ➜ ***worse***   *far* ➜ ***further***

Superlative adjectives

1 When we compare something with two or more other things, we use a superlative form with *the*.

*Steve is **the tallest** boy in our class.*
*Brazil is **the biggest** country in South America.*

2 With short adjectives, we normally add *-est*.

tall ➜ *the tall**est**   short* ➜ *the short**est***
old ➜ *the old**est**   clean* ➜ *the clean**est***

Spelling rules for the *-est* ending are the same as for the *-er* ending in the comparative form.

nice ➜ *the nic**est***   *happy* ➜ *the happ**iest***
safe ➜ *the saf**est***   *big* ➜ *the big**gest***
easy ➜ *the eas**iest***   *thin* ➜ *the thin**nest***

3 With longer adjectives (more than two syllables), we don't change the adjective – we put *the most* in front of it.

delicious ➜ ***the most*** *delicious*
important ➜ ***the most*** *important*
intelligent ➜ ***the most*** *intelligent*
*This is **the most important** day of my life.*

4 Some adjectives are irregular.

good ➜ ***the best***   *bad* ➜ ***the worst***   *far* ➜ ***the furthest***
*Saturday is **the best** day of the week.*
*My team is **the worst** team in the world!*

can / can't (ability)

1 We use *can / can't* + the base form of the verb to talk about someone's ability to do something. The form of *can / can't* is the same for every person.

*My father **can lift** 100 kg.*   *I **can't lift** heavy things.*
*I **can swim** 5 kilometres.*   *My brother **can't swim**.*

2 To make questions, we use *Can* + subject + base form of the verb. Short answers are formed with *Yes / No* + pronoun + *can* or *can't*.

***Can** your sister **swim**?   Yes, she **can**.*
***Can** you **lift** 50 kilos?   No, I **can't**.*

UNIT 10

be going to for plans and intentions

1 We use *be going to* to talk about things we intend to do in the future.

*I'm **going to visit** my grandfather tomorrow.*
*My sister's **going to study** German at university.*

2 The form is the present simple of *be* + *going to* + base form of the verb.

*I'm **going to stay** at home on Sunday. I'm **not going to go** out.*
*She's **going to look** around the shops. She **isn't going to buy** anything.*
***Are** you **going to watch** the film?*
***Is** he **going to give** us homework tonight?*

3 Short answers are formed using *Yes / No* + pronoun + the correct form of *be* (positive or negative).

Present continuous for future arrangements

We can use the present continuous to talk about arrangements for the future.

*We're **having** a party next weekend.* (It's organised.)
*I'm **meeting** my friends in the park tomorrow.* (I talked to my friends and we agreed to meet.)
*Our parents **are going** on holiday to Spain next month.* (They have their airline tickets and hotel reservation.)

Adverbs

1 Adverbs usually go with verbs – they describe an action.

*We **walked** home **slowly**.   The train **arrived late**.*
***Drive carefully**!*

2 A lot of adverbs are formed by adjective + *-ly*.

quiet ➜ *quietly*   *bad* ➜ *badly*   *polite* ➜ *politely*

If the adjective ends in *-le*, we drop the *-e* and add *-y*.

terrible ➜ *terribly*   *comfortable* ➜ *comfortably*

If the adjective ends in consonant + *-y*, we change the *-y* to *-i* and add *-ly*.

easy ➜ *easily*   *happy* ➜ *happily*   *lucky* ➜ *luckily*

3 Some adverbs are irregular – they don't have an *-ly* ending.

good ➜ *well*   *fast* ➜ *fast*   *hard* ➜ *hard*
early ➜ *early*   *late* ➜ *late*
*I played **well** last week.   He worked **hard** all day.*
*She ran very **fast**.*

4 Adverbs usually come immediately after the verb, or, if the verb has an object, after the object.

*She **sings well**.   She **plays the piano well**.*

UNIT 11
will / *won't* for future predictions

1 **We use *will* ('*ll*) and *won't* to make predictions about the future.**

*When I'm older, I'll **travel** round the world.*
*I **won't stay** here!*
*I'm sure you'll **pass** the test tomorrow. The questions **won't be** very difficult.*
*In the future, people **will take** holidays on Mars.*
*But people **won't live** there.*

2 **We use *will* / *won't* + base form of the verb, and the form is the same for all subjects. We don't use any form of *do* in the negative.**

*You'll **pass** the test.*   *You **won't pass** the test.*
*He'll **pass** the test.*   *He **won't pass** the test.*

3 **Questions are formed with *will* + subject + base form of the verb. Again, we don't use any form of *do* in questions or short answers.**

***Will** Andrea **go** to university?*
*Yes, she **will**. / No, she **won't**.*
***Will** your friends **come** to the party?*
*Yes, they **will**. / No, they **won't**.*

First conditional

1 **In conditional sentences there are two clauses, an *if* clause and a result clause. We use the first conditional when it is possible or likely that the situation in the *if* clause will happen in the future.**

*If I **pass** the test, my parents **will be** happy.*
(It's possible that I will pass, but I'm not sure.)
*If it **doesn't rain**, we'll **go** for a walk. (Perhaps it will rain, but I'm not sure.)*

2 **The *if* clause is formed with *if* + subject + present simple. The result clause is formed with subject + *will* + base form of the verb. There is a comma after the *if* clause.**

*If we **have** time, we'll **do** some shopping.*
*If you **don't start** your homework soon, you **won't finish** it tonight.*

3 **We can change the order of the two clauses. In this case, there is no comma between the clauses.**

*We'll **do** some shopping if we **have** time.*
*You **won't finish** your homework tonight if you **don't start** it soon.*

Time clauses with *when* / *as soon as*

In sentences about the future, we use the present tense after *when* or *as soon as*, and the *will* future in the main clause.

*When I'm 18, I'll **go** to university.*
*I'll **call** you as soon as I **get** there.*

UNIT 12
Present perfect simple with *ever* / *never*

1 **We often use the present perfect to talk about things from the beginning of our life until now.**

*Sandro **has travelled** to a lot of different countries. (from when he was born until now)*
*I **haven't met** your parents. (at any time in my life, from when I was born until now)*

2 **When we use the present perfect with this meaning, we often use *ever* (*at any time in someone's life*) in questions, and *never* (*not ever*) in sentences. *Ever* comes between the noun or pronoun and the past participle. *Never* comes immediately after *have* / *has*.**

***Have** you ever **eaten** Thai food?*
*I've never **been** interested in cooking.*

3 **The present perfect is formed with the present tense of *have* + past participle of the main verb. For regular verbs, the past participle has the same -ed ending as the past simple. Irregular verbs have different past participles.**

Regular verbs
*We've **stayed** in Athens three times.*
***Have** they ever **climbed** a mountain?*

Irregular verbs
*We've **been** there three times.*
***Have** they ever **flown** in a plane?*

See page 128 for the past participles of irregular verbs.

4 **There is a difference between *been* and *gone*.**

*I've **been** to the supermarket. (I went to the supermarket and now I am back again.)*
*They've **gone** to the supermarket. (They went to the supermarket and they are still there.)*

Present perfect vs. past simple

Both the present perfect and the past simple refer to the past. But we use the past simple to talk about situations or actions at a particular time in the past. We use the present perfect to talk about situations or actions in the past that took place at an unspecified time between the past and now.

Past simple
*I **ate** sushi **two weeks ago**.*
*I **read** a Shakespeare play **last month**.*
*He **was** late for school **yesterday**.*

Present perfect
*I've **eaten** sushi a lot of times.*
*I've **read** six Shakespeare plays.*
*He's **been** late to school four times.*

IRREGULAR VERBS

Base form	Past simple	Past participle
be	was / were	been
become	became	become
begin	began	begun
break	broke	broken
bring	brought	brought
build	built	built
buy	bought	bought
can	could	–
catch	caught	caught
choose	chose	chosen
come	came	come
cost	cost	cost
cut	cut	cut
do	did	done
draw	drew	drawn
drink	drank	drunk
drive	drove	driven
eat	ate	eaten
fall	fell	fallen
feel	felt	felt
find	found	found
fly	flew	flown
forget	forgot	forgotten
get	got	got
give	gave	given
go	went	gone
grow	grew	grown
have	had	had
hear	heard	heard
hit	hit	hit
keep	kept	kept
know	knew	known
leave	left	left

Base form	Past simple	Past participle
lend	lent	lent
lie	lay	lain
lose	lost	lost
make	made	made
mean	meant	meant
meet	met	met
pay	paid	paid
put	put	put
read /riːd/	read /red/	read /red/
ride	rode	ridden
run	ran	run
say	said	said
see	saw	seen
sell	sold	sold
send	sent	sent
show	showed	shown
sing	sang	sung
sit	sat	sat
sleep	slept	slept
speak	spoke	spoken
spend	spent	spent
stand	stood	stood
swim	swam	swum
take	took	taken
teach	taught	taught
tell	told	told
think	thought	thought
throw	threw	thrown
understand	understood	understood
wake	woke	woken
wear	wore	worn
win	won	won
write	wrote	written